Object Lessons
from Pebbles and Paper Clips

Object Lessons Series

Bess, C. W., *Children's Object Lessons from the Seasons*, 1026–8

Bess, C. W., *Object-Centered Children's Sermons*, 0734–8

Bess, C. W., *Sparkling Object Sermons for Children*, 0824–7

Bess, C. W., & Roy DeBrand, *Bible-Centered Object Sermons for Children*, 0886–7

Biller, Tom & Martie, *Simple Object Lessons for Children*, 0793–3

Bruinsma, Sheryl, *Easy-to-Use Object Lessons*, 0832–8

Bruinsma, Sheryl, *More Object Lessons for Very Young Children*, 1075–6

Bruinsma, Sheryl, *New Object Lessons*, 0775–5

Bruinsma, Sheryl, *Object Lessons for Every Occasion*, 0994–4

Bruinsma, Sheryl, *Object Lessons for Special Days*, 0920–0

Bruinsma, Sheryl, *Object Lessons for Very Young Children*, 0956–1

Claassen, David, *Object Lessons for a Year*, 2514–1

Connelly, H. W., *47 Object Lessons for Youth Programs*, 2314–9

Coombs, Robert, *Concise Object Sermons for Children*, 2541–9

Coombs, Robert, *Enlightening Object Lessons for Children*, 2567–2

Cooper, Charlotte, *50 Object Stories for Children*, 2523–0

Cross, Luther, *Easy Object Stories*, 2502–8

Cross, Luther, *Object Lessons for Children*, 2315–7

Cross, Luther, *Story Sermons for Children*, 2328–9

De Jonge, Joanne, *More Object Lessons from Nature*, 3004–8

De Jonge, Joanne, *Object Lessons from Nature*, 2989–9

De Jonge, Joanne, *Object Lessons from Your Home and Yard*, 3026–9

Edstrom, Lois, *Contemporary Object Lessons for Children's Church*, 3432–9

Gebhardt, Richard, & Mark Armstrong, *Object Lessons from Science Experiments*, 3811–1

Godsey, Kyle, *Object Lessons About God*, 3841–3

Hendricks, William, *Object Lessons Based on Bible Characters*, 4373–5

Hendricks, William, & Merle Den Bleyker, *Object Lessons from Sports and Games*, 4134–1

Hendricks, William, & Merle Den Bleyker, *Object Lessons That Teach Bible Truths*, 4172–4

Loeks, Mary, *Object Lessons for Children's Worship*, 5584–9

McDonald, Roderick, *Successful Object Sermons*, 6270–5

Runk, Wesley, *Object Lessons from the Bible*, 7698–6

Squyres, Greg, *Simple Object Lessons for Young Children*, 8330–3

Sullivan, Jessie, *Object Lessons and Stories for Children's Church*, 8037–1

Sullivan, Jessie, *Object Lessons with Easy-to-Find Objects*, 8190–4

Trull, Joe, *40 Object Sermons for Children*, 8831–3

Object Lessons
from Pebbles and Paper Clips

Joanne E. De Jonge

Baker Books

A Division of Baker Book House Co
Grand Rapids, Michigan 49516

©1995 by Joanne E. De Jonge

Published by Baker Books
a division of Baker Book House Company
P.O. Box 6287, Grand Rapids, MI 49516-6287

ISBN 0–8010–5041–3

Printed in the United States of America

This book is dedicated to
JESUS.
"Let the little children come to me . . ."

Contents

Introduction

You can always find a pebble or a paper clip. All objects used in this book are common. You can pick them up easily before the lesson, and the children will see them often to recall the lesson.

As another aid to recall, a song has been suggested for use with many of the lessons. Have you ever had a familiar tune replay itself in your head? That's the idea. If the children know the suggested song, you may want to use it for background music at some point. Or you may want to sing it together. Or you may not want to use it at all. It's included as an option.

Other options are included in several lessons. You'll find some highlighted with a note and some under "option" headings. Every situation is different; the options may give you some ideas. They give you more flexibility on when, where, and how you present these object lessons.

How you present these lessons is ultimately determined by your own style. If you are a rank beginner and feel you have no unique style yet, the stage directions are included for you, italicized, in parentheses. You can take each lesson literally. If you're an old hand, you can simply use the ideas from each lesson.

Several lessons include special ideas for presentation or for recall. Most are as simple as adopting a pebble or pocketing a paper clip. Many aren't highlighted in any way; you'll find them as you read the lesson.

Page through the book. Check the objects, recall a song or two, note the options, consider the stage directions, and mull over the ideas. Then use them to teach biblical truths the children will recall whenever they see pebbles or paper clips. That's the whole idea.

1

Precious Pebbles

Scripture: For I am the LORD your God, . . .
I have . . . covered you with the shadow of
my hand (Isa. 51:15–16).

Concept: God holds us in the hollow of his
hands.

Objects: One pebble for each child and one for
you. (*Note:* If you plan to use "Know Your
Pebble" next week, collect two pebbles per
person. If pebbles aren't available, you can
use any other natural object.)

Song: "Safe Am I."

I've got something very precious for you
today. Hold out your hands like this *(cup your hands)*
to be sure you won't drop it.

(Continue to speak as you pass out the pebbles.) You'll
probably notice right away that I'm giving each of
you a pebble. You may think that a pebble isn't very
precious, but we're going to pretend that it is. Pretend that I'm passing out very precious pebbles. You
each get one precious stone; be sure to protect it. Let
it rest in your hand. Don't drop it. Be very careful.

*(Continue to talk about how careful they should be
and how precious their pebbles are until each child has*

one. Then resume your normal place, holding your pebble in your cupped hands.)

Take a close look at your pebble. *(Bring it close to your face.)* Beautiful, isn't it? Pretend for a minute that someone else wants to take your precious pebble. Watch out, they're looking at it and want to snatch it away! *(Cover your pebble with one hand.)* How can you protect your pebble? *(Pause for response.)* That's right, you can cover it with your hands.

Now, pretend that you have to keep your precious pebble warm. What will you do? *(Slowly cover your pebble with one hand and wait for response.)* Yes! You'll cover it with your hands and hold it close.

Now it's raining, and that pebble must not get wet. What will you do? *(Pause for response.)* Yes! Keep it covered and hold it close.

Let's put our pebbles on the floor *(Put your pebble on the floor. Pause while they set their pebbles down.)* Can you protect your pebble or keep it safe, warm, and dry when it's on the floor? *(Pause for response.)* Not really. If you want to take good care of your pebble you'll hold it in your hands.

Pick it up and protect it. *(Pick your pebble up and cup your hands around it.)* There, that's the way to protect something so precious. That's the way God protects us. He tells us that he covers us with his hands.

God doesn't really have hands, does he? *(Pause for response.)* No, he doesn't. But we do. God uses those words so that we will understand him. He says that we are so precious to him that he covers us with his hands. *(Hold up your hands protecting your pebble as you speak. Then bring them in close to you.)* That way God keeps each one of us close to him.

Option 1

(If you are going to use "Know Your Pebble," finish with the following paragraphs.)

Look at your precious pebble again. *(Uncover your hands and look closely at your pebble.)* You may keep your precious pebble this week. Take good care of it.

Don't lose it, because I want you to bring it back next week. Keep it in a safe place when you can't hold it. Once in a while pick it up and look at it closely. *(Demonstrate.)* Get to know what it looks like and what it feels like. This is your precious pebble. Every time you hold it this week, you can think about how God holds you in his hands.

You may take your pebble back to your seat now. Cover it with your hands *(demonstrate)* to protect it. Keep it safe and bring it back next week. And may God keep you safe in his hands and bring you back next week.

Option 2

(If you are not going to use "Know Your Pebble," finish with the following paragraph.)

Look at your precious pebble one more time. *(Uncover your hands and look closely at your pebble.)* What a precious pebble you have! You may keep your precious pebble. Cover it with your hands as you go back to your seats. Take good care of it. Protect it, because it's your very own precious pebble. It can remind you that you are God's very own precious child. He holds you close to him in the hollow of his hands.

lem. I've brought some extra pebbles with me. Hold out your hands *(demonstrate with cupped hands)* if you need a pebble.

(Review last week's lesson as you pass out pebbles.) These are very precious pebbles, aren't they? Show me how you protect something precious. *(Pause while they demonstrate.)* That's right. Who protects us with his hands? *(Pause for response.)* Yes, God does! We are so precious to him that he holds us in his hands *(pick up your pebble and protect it)* just the way we hold our precious pebbles. We talked about that last week.

Open your hands and look closely at your precious pebble while I'm talking. Look at its color. Is it black, white, tan? Remember what color it is. Does it have stripes, or patches of other color? Look at its shape. Is it round? Does it have rough edges? Does it have little bumps or little holes in it? If we put all our pebbles together, would you be able to find your one precious pebble? Roll it over in your hands and look at it closely, because we are going to put them all together in a minute. Get to know your pebble, because you're going to have to rescue it.

Do you know your own pebble? Could you pick it out of a crowd? *(Collect the pebbles. Continue speaking as you do so.)* I'll take your pebbles now, but just for a minute. *(Put all the pebbles together in the middle of the circle.)* Look at the pile of pebbles. They all look quite a bit alike, don't they? Somewhere in there is your special pebble. Will you be able to find it?

Pretend that your precious pebble is calling for you, and you want to rescue it. We'll each try to rescue our own pebble. We probably won't be able to pick our own pebbles out of that crowd, but we

16

won't worry if we can't find it. There are enough pebbles for all of us. Still, it would be nice to find our special pebble, so we'll try.

You can look for your pebble now. *(Spread the pile of pebbles and look for yours. Encourage the children to look for theirs for about a minute.)* There! If you don't have your own pebble, that's OK. Just take any pebble and sit down. *(Make sure each child has a pebble; then help them form a circle again.)*

Look at the pebble you have. Is it your own precious pebble? *(Pause for response.)* Good! Some of us have our pebbles, but not all of us. It's just too hard to tell one pebble from another. Maybe we didn't know our pebbles well enough, so we got them mixed up with other pebbles.

Do you think that God can ever get you mixed up with other people? You protected your pebble in your hands, just the way God protects you in his hands. But then, you lost your pebble in the crowd. Can God lose you in a crowd like that? *(Pause for response.)*

No! Of course not! God never, ever loses you in a crowd. You are so precious to God that he knows all about you. The Bible says that God knows when you sit down, when you get up, when you sleep, when you wake. You are so precious to God that he is always watching you. *(Peer closely at your pebble and continue to speak.)* He even knows what you're going to say before you say it. God loves you so much that he never takes his eyes off you.

Of course we lost our pebbles. It's hard to tell the difference among pebbles. And maybe we didn't really love our pebbles enough to care. But God loves you enough to care. He cares for you much more than any of us cared for our old pebbles.

You may take your new pebble home. Hold it in the hollow of your hand. And when you do, remember that God holds you in his hands and watches you. You are his precious child. He knows all about you and will never, ever lose you in a crowd.

3

Paper Clip Christians

Scripture: Jesus replied, "If anyone loves me, he will obey my teaching" (John 14:23).

In the same way, faith by itself, if it is not accompanied by action, is dead (James 2:17).

Concept: Christians put love into action.

Objects: Paper clips (at least one for each child), a few sheets of paper.

Can you see these? *(Hold up a few paper clips.)* What are they? *(Pause for response.)* Of course, they're paper clips. *(Hold up a paper clip.)* Its name tells us what this little thing is, doesn't it? This is a paper clip. It clips paper together.

What are paper clips for? What do they do? *(Pause for response.)* Yes, they hold pieces of paper together.

(Hold up the sheets of paper.) I want to keep these together. They could very easily become separated, like this. *(Demonstrate.)* If I use a paper clip *(put a paper clip on them)*, I'll keep them together.

(Hold up the box or envelope containing the clips.) Paper clips don't do much good in here, do they? They usually get all tangled together in the box (envelope). *(Take out a mass of clips.)* What a bother! They don't do any good like this.

But when they do what they're meant to do *(hold up the papers clipped together),* they're very useful.

In a way, all of us Christians are like these paper clips. That sounds funny, doesn't it? Let me explain.

First of all, the name *Christian* says exactly what we are. If we are Christians, we are followers of Jesus *Christ.* Christians are people who love Jesus *Christ.*

And just like paper clips, Christians have a purpose. Jesus said, "If anyone loves me, he will obey my teaching." Christians obey Jesus Christ.

Can anyone remember what Jesus taught us? Jesus said that we should love God and do what to others? *(Pause for response.)* How about love? Jesus said that we should love God and love other as ourselves.

What can we *do* to show love? *(Pause for response. Repeat their responses. You may have to prompt them with questions using action verbs.)* Can we share our toys with others? Can we obey our parents? Can we avoid quarrels? Can we tell others about Jesus? Can we help out around the house? Can we give to others cheerfully?

You've got the idea. There are lots of things we can do to show that we are Christians. There are lots of ways to show love to others.

Do you think Jesus wants us just to *say,* "I love you," or does he want us to *do* things to show love? *(Pause for response.)* That's right, he wants us to *do* loving things. If we don't *do* anything to show love, if we just say, "I love you," we're sort of like these paper clips all jumbled together *(hold up a string of jumbled paper clips),* aren't we? We're just sitting together not doing what we're meant to do.

(Take one clip out of the jumble and put it on the papers.) But if we show love by our actions, we're

obeying Jesus' command to love. Then we're acting as Christians should.

(Pass out the paper clips. Continue to speak as you do so.) I've got some paper clips for you today. I'd like you to do something with your paper clip this week.

Take your paper clip home with you and try to keep it with you this whole week. Put it in a pocket so that you always have it with you. At night, take it out of your pocket and put it where you can notice it the next morning. Then, when you get dressed, put it back into a pocket. That way, you'll carry your paper clip all week long.

Every time you put your hand into your pocket, you'll feel that paper clip. That can remind you about how Christians are like paper clips. The paper clip isn't doing a whole lot of good in your pocket, just as we don't do a whole lot of good if we just talk about love. So, every time you feel your paper clip, try to *act* out a little love. Be a working paper clip Christian. Show someone that you love them.

Real True Love

Scripture: God is love (1 John 4:8).

Concept: God loves us.

Objects: Valentines, enough so that every child can have one. (*Note:* If you purchase valentines and plan to do "Love Each Other" at some time, purchase twice as many as you need and put half of them in a safe place.)

Song: "Jesus Loves Me."

Who can tell me what this is? *(Hold up a valentine. Pause for response.)* You're right! It's a valentine. We see a lot of them this time of the year, don't we?

(Hold up a valentine that has a heart on the front.) Most valentines have hearts on them someplace. What does a heart remind us of, hate or love? *(Pause for response.)* Of course, a heart reminds us of love.

That's why most valentines have hearts on them. People use valentines to tell one another that they love each other.

Some of these valentines are really serious things, aren't they? *(Read a few valentines.)* Some are funny, some are cute, some are just kind of nice—a little reminder that someone is thinking of you.

Did you notice something? I didn't even say love that time. People often send valentines to other people just to make them feel happy and good. Valentines don't always mean, "Oh, I love you so much." Sometimes they just mean, "I love you like a friend" or "I really like you a lot." That's OK. It's still nice to get valentines, isn't it?

You probably won't get a valentine from someone who says, "I love you so much that I want to be with you forever. I'll never, ever, leave you—never! I'll always always love you—no matter what you do—with a real, true love!" No one gets a valentine like that, do they? *(Shake your head and pause for response.)*

Well, I've got a surprise for you! Each one of you is getting a valentine like that, right here today! *(Pass out the valentines as you speak.)*

In fact, you've got a valentine like that already. It's just not printed out on a fancy little card like this. It's printed in the Bible.

So these little valentines are going to remind you of the real valentine in the Bible. The Bible says that God loves you perfectly—with a real, true love. In fact, the Bible says that God *is* love. And God, who loves you so much, promised always to be with you and to never, ever leave you.

These valentines don't say those words, do they? These valentines are just to remind you that God loves you, with a real, true love. So, we're going to look at them and just pretend that each one says, "God loves me." Can you remember that?

Let's practice a minute. What does your valentine say? God loves me. *(Say it slowly enough so some chil-*

dren can join you.) What does your valentine say? *(Pause for response, or say it with the children.)*

You may take your very special valentine home with you today. I'd like you to try something with it. Put it up where you can see it—in your bedroom or on the refrigerator—and every time you look at it, say, "God loves me."

You may see lots of other valentines around right now, but this is your special valentine. The other ones may get lost or thrown away very soon, but I'd like you to see how long you can keep this special valentine. Keep it right in sight to remind you that God loves you. But also keep it there for a long, long time, to remind you that God will love you forever.

Option

(If you plan to do "Love Each Other," you may want to add the following paragraph.)

In fact, sometime, several months from now, I'm going to ask you if you still have your special valentine. You will always have the promise from God. But just to see if you can remember it, let's see how long you can keep this little valentine, this reminder. If you lose it, don't worry. God will still love you forever!

5

Love Each Other

Scripture: Dear friends, since God so loved us, we also ought to love one another (1 John 4:11).

Concept: We should love each other.

Objects: Valentines, one for each child. (*Note:* This is a companion to "Real, True Love." If you have done that, use the valentines you have saved. If you haven't, draw a heart on a piece of paper for each child and use option 1.)

Song: "They'll Know We Are Christians By Our Love."

Option 1

What's this? (*Hold up a paper with a heart drawn on it. Pause for response.*) Yes, it's a heart.

What does a heart remind us of, hate or love? (*Pause for response.*) Of course, a heart reminds us of love.

Who, do you think, loves you more than anyone in the world? (*Pause for response. Repeat any response.*) Your parents? Of course, your parents love you very much. But who loves you even more than your parents? Yes, God.

The Bible tells us that God is love. God loves you very, very much and has said that he will always, always love you.

We often use a heart to remind us of love. And the best love of all is God's love for us. The Bible tells us that.

Option 2

(If you have done "Real, True Love," say,) How many of you recognize this? *(Hold up a valentine. Pause for response.)* Yes, it's a valentine! You don't see many valentines right now; stores aren't selling them. But you did a few months ago. In fact, I gave you each a valentine then, and I asked you to keep it as long as you could.

How many of you still have that valentine I gave you? *(Raise your hand as you ask the question and pause for response.)* Some of you still have it. Good for you! If you lost it, that's no problem. You all still have the promise of that valentine.

Who can remember what that valentine said? *(Pause for response. You may have to prompt them with a few questions.)* It said something about love. Who loves you? Who promised never to leave you? The Bible says that who is love? Yes! God is love. God loves you very much. That's what we said when we passed out those valentines.

We wanted to remind ourselves that God loves us and will always love us. The Bible tells us that.

Continue Lesson

But the Bible tells us more that that. It goes on to say that, since God loves us, we ought to love . . .

whom should we love? *(Pause for response and repeat their responses.)* Our parents? Yes! Our brothers and sisters? Of course! What about you and me? Should I love you and you love me? Yes! The Bible says that since God loves us, we also ought to love one another. We should love everybody that's here today!

How can you show people that you love them? *(Pause for response. Repeat their responses.)* Can you always be pleasant to them? Sure! Can you help them when they need help? Of course! Can you share with them? Yes! When you love someone, you're as nice as you can be to them.

That's not always easy to do, is it? Sometimes we just feel grumpy. Or sometimes the other person is grumpy. Our love isn't as good as God's love. We don't always love each other. But we keep on trying. We try to be nice and loving, even when we're grumpy or someone else is grumpy.

That's not always easy to remember, is it? Sometimes, when we're grumpy, we forget about love. God never forgets about love. God *is* love. We forget, because we're not God. Yet the Bible tells us that because God loves us, we should love each other.

So, I have something to help you remember to love each other this week. I have a valentine (*or a heart*) for each of you. *(Pass out the valentines or hearts. Continue to speak as you do so.)*

We're going to pretend that these valentines (hearts) say, "Love each other." OK? Let's practice. What do these hearts say? Love each other. *(Say it slowly so that the children can join you.)* What does your heart say? *(Pause for response.)* Love each other!

6

Who Shows the Way?

Scripture: I will instruct you and teach you in the way you should go (Ps. 32:8).

Concept: God will guide us through life.

Object: A picture of a robin.

Song: "Lead Me, Guide Me."

I have a picture with me today; I didn't want to catch this little creature. I figured that a picture can remind us well enough. *(Hold up the picture.)* What is it? *(Pause for response.)* That's right, it's a bird. Look at the red belly. What kind of bird is it? *(Pause for response.)* Yes, it's a robin! I saw a robin this week and brought a picture along to remind us of robins.

Has anyone seen a robin lately? *(Raise your hand as you ask the question.)* If you haven't, you probably will soon, because they've returned. Most of them were gone all winter, but they're back now. Lots of birds are returning for the summer.

Where do these birds go during winter, does anyone know? *(Pause for response.)* Yes, they fly south. Sometimes they go a long, long way. They'll fly for days to reach their winter homes. And they'll fly for days to come back here. Some birds come back to exactly the same yard, or field, or woods, or nest every year.

How do the birds find their way? They don't have maps. There are no highway signs in the sky. Who shows them the way? *(Pause for response.)* That's right, God shows them the way.

God doesn't take each bird and whisper in its ear, does he? And he doesn't tie a string to each bird to lead it to the right place. We don't understand how birds find the right place. We just know that's the way God made them. He shows them the way to go by somehow putting the right directions into their bodies.

God said that he would show us the way to go, too. He said, "I will instruct you and teach you in the way you should go."

Does that mean that God will give you directions to get home from church or to go to your friend's house tomorrow? *(Pause for response.)* Of course not! Much better than that, God has promised to guide us through life.

God has promised to help us live right, to make right choices, to do the right things. He said that he would show the way we should go, how we should live.

How does God guide us? How does he tell us the way to live? *(Pause for response. Repeat each response with a positive comment. If responses aren't forthcoming, lead them with a few questions.)* That's right, God gives us parents to help guide us. He gives us the Bible to tell us right and wrong. We should listen to our parents, read our Bibles, and pray to God. And he will let us know how we should live; he will guide us through life.

That's sort of like this bird *(hold up the picture)*, isn't it? God leads this bird for hundreds of miles. There are no signs or maps; we can't see God guide the bird, but he does. So God leads us through our lives. He doesn't shout at us, he doesn't put up big signs about right and wrong, but he still leads us. Through the Bible and prayer and our parents, God guides us through life.

This week, try to see how many robins you can count. Whenever you see one, say a little prayer. Ask God, who guides the robin, to guide you through your life. He's promised to do that.

7

God's Favorite Color

Scripture: I now realize how true it is that God does not show favoritism but accepts men from every nation who fear him and do what is right (Acts 10:34–35).

Concept: God loves people of all colors.

Object: None, if the children can see the outdoors from where they are seated (Option 1). If you are not near a window, use a simple, colored picture of the outdoors. (*Note:* This lesson is designed for use in churches that are not very diverse ethnically.)

Song: "Jesus Loves the Little Children."

Option 1

I didn't bring anything with me today because God put it in place long ago. All we have to do is look out of the window.

Option 2

(*If you have a picture, say,*) Since we can't go outside right now, I brought a picture of the outdoors inside. (*Hold up the picture.*) This can help us think about trees and the sky and things like that.

Continue Lesson

Let's talk for a minute about the colors that God put into the outdoors. There are so many of them; we can see only a few from here.

Look at the sky. What's one color that you usually see outdoors during the day? *(Pause for response.)* Blue! Sometimes the sky is a deep blue, sometimes it's gray. But it's usually some sort of blue. It's that way all over the world. God must really like blue. He used a lot of blue outdoors.

Look at the trees and grass. What's another color that you always see outdoors? *(Pause for response.)* Green! Green is really important outside. It's the color of grass and bushes and leaves and plants. There are all different shades of green outside, and there's always some green out there. God must really like green. He used a lot of green outdoors.

What do you think is God's favorite color for the outdoors, blue or green? *(Pause briefly for response.)* It's difficult to know, isn't it? God used a lot of blue and green outdoors.

But then, maybe yellow is God's favorite color, and he saved it for the flowers. He put yellow dandelions all over the world. They always add a beautiful touch. Maybe he likes yellow best of all for the outdoors.

Or how about red? Do you think God's favorite color for the outdoors is red? Think about juicy red apples, or beautiful red flowers, or gorgeous red birds, or cute little ladybugs. Maybe God likes red best of all outdoors, so he saved it for the really special things.

God used so many colors in nature, and he didn't tell us about favorites. Maybe it doesn't matter. Maybe it's blue or green, because there's a lot of those colors. Or maybe he saved his favorite color for little bits here and there. It's hard to tell if God has a favorite color for the outdoors.

How about people? Do you think that God has a favorite color for people? Look at all the people in church today. Do you see lots of different colors in faces or mostly one color? *(Pause for response.)* We have mostly one color in our church, don't we? Our church is mostly white *(or whatever it is)*. Maybe God's favorite color for people is white. He used a lot of white in this church.

But pretend for a minute that you're sitting in a church halfway around the world, in Africa. Would you see a lot of white? *(Shake your head as you pause for response.)* No! You'd see a lot of black. Then you might think that God's favorite color for people is black.

If you were sitting in India, you'd see a lot of brown. You might think, or people in India might think, that God's favorite color is brown. In China, you might think that God's favorite people-color is yellow.

Look at all the people in church again. Pretend that there are a few *(or* Look at the*)* faces of different colors here. Maybe God likes those colors so much that he saved them for very special people! Maybe those are God's favorite people-colors. It's hard to tell, isn't it?

It really *isn't* hard to tell what God's favorite color for people is, because he told us. In the Bible God says that he has no favorites. He loves people from all nations. God loves people of all colors. The Bible says that he does.

It is important to know that God doesn't have a favorite people-color. That's why he told us. He wants to be sure that we know. Any person of any color can be his child. He loves us all; color doesn't make any difference to him. And color shouldn't make any difference to us.

It isn't important to know if God has a favorite color for the outdoors. *(Hold up the picture or point to the window.)* There are lots of pretty colors out there. If God has a favorite outdoor-color, it doesn't matter. We know that he does *not* have a favorite people-color, and that's what matters.

I'd like you to try something on your way home from church today. Try to count all the colors that you see outdoors. See if you have a favorite outdoor-color.

Then try to see how many different people-colors you can find. Whenever you see a person colored differently from you, tell yourself that the different color doesn't make a difference to God. God told us that he has no favorites. He loves people of every color.

8

Blessed Showers

Scripture: He covers the sky with clouds; he supplies the earth with rain and makes grass grow on the hills (Ps. 147:8). Also: Deut. 11:14; 28:12; Job 5:6; Ps. 68:9; Zech. 10:1. (*Note:* You may want to copy these verses on a sheet for you to read and copy a verse for each child to take home.)

Concept: Life-giving rain is a blessing from God.

Object: None, if you can see rain from inside (option 1). If you can't, use a drawing of rain coming from a cloud. (*Note:* This can be done any time, but works best on a rainy day. It can be used during a rainy season a week before the lesson "Showers of Blessing.")

Song: "Showers of Blessing" or "Dropping, Dropping, Falls the Rain" (also called "Sun and Rain").

Option 1

What's the weather like outside? Is it nice and sunny, or is it raining again? *(Pause for response.)* Yes, it's raining. *(Point to the window or hold up the picture. Try to look quite gloomy as you speak.)* It's been raining for quite a while now, hasn't it? Gray skies, lots of water; it looks like we're going to have more rain.

Option 2

(If it's sunny, say,) What's the weather like outside? is it sunny or rainy? *(Pause for response.)* Good! It's a nice, sunny day. I'm glad it isn't raining.

Continue Lesson

Sometimes I get tired of rainy days, don't you? *(Pause for response.)* I get tired of staying inside, and always using an umbrella, and getting wet anyway, and postponing picnics, and looking at gray clouds instead of the sun. Rainy days often make me feel as gray as the weather. Do they do that to you, too? *(Pause for response.)* I think it's natural to feel gray on rainy days. Sometimes it's hard to thank the Lord for rain.

(Brighten up a bit.) But that's exactly what we should do. We should thank the Lord for this rain. Rain is really a blessing that God sends us. We need rain. Rain is a good thing.

Think about the grass on your lawn and the flowers in your garden. Do they need water? *(Pause for response.)* Of course they do! They would die without water, so God sends rain. That's how God waters his plants.

How about all the food we eat, the things that farmers grow? Do potatoes and rice and apples and oranges need water? *(Pause for response.)* Of course they do! They would die without water, so God sends rain.

How about all the creatures outside, the birds, the squirrels, the rabbits, even our cows and horses? Think about fish. Do they need water? *(Pause for response.)*

Of course they do! Everything needs water, so God sends rain. Without the water that God sends as rain, we couldn't live. So rain is a blessing from God.

Of course, we don't want too much rain, do we? We don't want floods. But usually God stops the rain before there's too much. Usually, rain is a blessing, a good thing, that God gives us.

The Bible talks over and over again about how good rain is.

Option 3

(If you have the verses listed, say,) There are so many verses I had to write them down. This is what the Bible says about rain. *(Read the verses.)*

Option 4

(If you don't have the verses listed, say,) God promised to send the Israelites rain as a blessing. During seasons that were too dry, they prayed to God to send rain. The Bible often talks about how God sends rain to make plants grow. It talks about rain as a blessing from God.

Continue Lesson

But you still have to stay inside when it rains, don't you? *(Pause for response.)* You may know that rain is a good thing, but you still have to play inside or get all soggy if you go outside. That will never change.

But maybe your mood can change. Maybe, now that you know we need rain and it's a blessing from

God, you can smile a bit about it. Instead of saying *(put on a gloomy face)*, "Ugh, it's raining," you can say *(put on a happy face)*, "Oh well, we need rain. Thank you, God." Try that if it rains this week. Think of rain as something good, and thank God for it.

Option 5

(If you have a verse for each child, say,) I have something to help you. On each of these papers *(show the papers)* is a verse from the Bible about how good rain is. Take it home with you and keep it in a safe place. Then, every time it rains, take out the verse and have someone read it to you. It will remind you that rain is a good thing God gives us.

Showers of Blessing

Scripture: I will send down showers in season; there will be showers of blessing (Ezek. 34:26).

Concept: God sends us more blessings than we can count.

Object: A drawing of many raindrops coming from a cloud. (*Note:* This can be done any time, but works best on a rainy day. It can be used during a rainy season the week after the lesson "Blessed Showers." If it's rainy, use option 1.)

Song: "Showers of Blessing," "Count Your Blessings, Name Them One by One."

Option 1

What's the weather like outside? Is it nice and sunny, or is it raining again? (*Pause for response.*) Yes, it's raining. (*Point to the window or hold up the picture. Try to look quite gloomy as you speak.*) It's been raining for quite a while now, hasn't it? Gray skies, lots of water; it looks like we're going to have some more rain.

Option 2

(If it's sunny, say,) What's the weather like outside? Is it sunny or rainy? *(Pause for response.)* Good! It's a nice, sunny day. I'm glad it isn't raining.

Continue Lesson

Sometimes it's hard to know what to do on rainy days, isn't it? *(Pause for response.)* When it rains all day and you have to play inside, sometimes you run out of things to do, don't you? *(Pause for response.)* Does this sound familiar *(use a whining voice)*: "There's nothing to do in here. What can I do?" *(Pause for response.)* I think we all feel like that at times on rainy days.

Well, I have something for you to do today *(or on the next rainy day)*. Try to count raindrops! Stand next to a window and count all the raindrops that hit the window. Or look outside and try to count every raindrop you see fall.

Let's try to count the raindrops in this picture. *(Hold up the picture. Point to the drops and count slowly, so the children can count with you.)* One, two, three, four . . . oh well, let's not count them all. There are too many to count.

Do you think you could count real raindrops? *(Pause for response.)* Probably not; there usually are too many to count. But it might be fun to try. If you try, all that counting can remind you of God's blessings, of the good things that God gives us.

What in the world do God's blessings have to do with rain? Well, God compares his blessings to showers. God says that he will send us showers of blessing. That means he'll give us so many good things that we can't even count them. Just like raindrops, there are too many blessings to count.

And just like counting raindrops, we can try to count God's blessings anyway. Let's try. Look around this room (*or* church), and see how many blessings you can count. I'll get you started. *(Point to things as you mention them.)* One: How about lights? They're good things, blessings from God. Two: How about the seats? Would you like to sit on the floor? Seats are another blessing. Three: Look at your parents. They're certainly a good thing from God. Four: Don't forget your friends. Five: Is the pastor a blessing? *(Continue until you feel time running out. Encourage the children to name blessings they can see. Mention physical aspects of the building, people and relationships, things the children are wearing, body parts, etc. Try to end with the Bible and all its promises.)*

I think you get the idea, don't you? God gives us so many good things, so many blessings, that we simply can't count them.

That's just like raindrops. There are too many to count.

So, the next time it rains (*or* since it's raining today) and you must stay inside, you'll have something new and fun to do. Try to count the raindrops. When you give up, try to name, then count your blessings. That could keep you busy all day.

10

The Best Symbol of All

Scripture: May I never boast except in the cross of our Lord Jesus Christ (Gal. 6:14).

Concept: A cross is a symbol for Jesus.

Objects: Drawn pictures of the sun (with rays), a crescent moon, a heart, yellow McDonald's arches, and a cross. Each should be on a separate sheet of paper.

Song: "In the Cross of Christ I Glory."

I brought some symbols with me today so that we could talk about them. A symbol is a picture that stands for something.

(*Show the sun.*) What's this? (*Pause for response.*) Of course, it's the sun. You can tell by those sunbeams coming out of it. Is it really the sun? (*Pause for response.*) Of course not. It's a picture of the sun. We look at it and think of the sun.

If you saw this anyplace you would probably recognize it as the sun. It could be up on a wall; it doesn't have to be on a piece of paper, does it? It's a picture of the sun. We could almost call it a symbol.

(*Show the moon.*) What's this? (*Pause for response.*) Yes, it's a picture of the moon. It's not the real thing, yet it makes us think of the real thing. It stands for the moon.

Here's a good symbol. (*Show the heart.*) What's this? (*Pause for response.*) Sure, it's a heart. It isn't a real heart. It isn't even a good picture of a real heart. A real heart isn't shaped like this. But we use hearts shaped like this when we want to show . . . (*Pause for response.*) Sure, we use a heart to show love. When we look at this heart, it reminds us of love. This is a symbol for love.

Here's another symbol (*hold up the arches*): golden arches. Does that give you a clue? Does McDonald's have golden arches? (*Pause for response.*) Every McDonald's fast food place has golden arches like this, I think. So these golden arches have become a symbol. When people look at them, they think of McDonald's, and then they think of fast food. These arches are a symbol for McDonald's fast food.

Now I've got the best symbol of all. (*Hold up the cross.*) What's this? (*Pause for response.*) Yes, it's a cross. It's really a picture of a cross. Christians often use this symbol, don't they?

(*If there are crosses in the sanctuary, ask the children to point them out.*)

I said that the cross was the best symbol of all. Let's find out why.

First of all, what's a symbol? (*Pause for response.*) That's right. A symbol is a picture that stands for something. (*Show the pictures.*) These are symbols of the sun, the moon, love, and McDonald's.

(*Hold up the cross.*) What does this picture stand for? (*Pause for response. You may have to lead them with questions.*) Does it stand for a real cross? Who died on a real cross to save us from our sins? Jesus did! Anytime you see a cross, think of Jesus. The cross is a symbol for Jesus.

The best thing that ever happened to us happened when Jesus died on the cross to save us. So the cross *(hold up the picture)* is the best symbol of all.

Maybe you won't remember the word "symbol," but you can always remember this. *(Hold up the picture.)* This is a symbol for who? *(Pause for response.)* Jesus! Whenever you see a cross, you can think of Jesus. This is the best symbol of all.

11

No More Caterpillars

Scripture: Therefore, if anyone is in Christ, he is a new creation; the old has gone, the new has come! (2 Cor. 5:17).

Concept: God sees Christians as beautiful creatures.

Objects: A butterfly and a drawing of a caterpillar. (*Note:* A drawing of a butterfly will do if the wings are colored brightly.)

Song: "If I Were a Butterfly."

I brought along one of the most beautiful creatures on earth. *(Show the butterfly.)* Can you think of anything prettier than a butterfly? I can't. Look at those wings—the bright colors and the pretty patterns. Who likes butterflies? *(Raise your hand as you ask, to encourage a like response.)* I do, too. I think everyone likes butterflies; they're so delicate and pretty.

This wasn't always a butterfly, was it? Who knows what this was before it became a butterfly? *(Pause for response.)* Yes, it was a caterpillar! *(Show the picture of the caterpillar.)* This is an entirely different creature, isn't it?

(During the next paragraph, hold up either the butterfly or the picture of the caterpillar as you talk about them. Don't hold them side by side.)

This butterfly was once a caterpillar somewhat like this. But then, at some point in its life, it changed into this beautiful butterfly. We can't explain how a caterpillar becomes a butterfly; only God knows that. We just know that a caterpillar becomes a butterfly.

(During the next three paragraphs, hold the butterfly and the picture of the caterpillar side by side and indicate each one as you talk about it.)

A caterpillar isn't nearly as pretty as a butterfly, is it? It usually doesn't have the beautiful colors of a butterfly.

Can a caterpillar fly? *(Pause for response.)* Of course not! A caterpillar crawls along the ground, or up a tree, or sometimes on your house. A butterfly floats on the breeze, flitting between flowers.

What does a caterpillar eat? *(Pause for response.)* Yes, a caterpillar eats leaves, lots of leaves. In fact, too many caterpillars can kill a tree or bush by eating all its leaves. Does a butterfly eat leaves? *(Pause for response.)* No! It drinks nectar from flowers. It never harms the flowers, and it never harms trees or bushes.

If I were a caterpillar, I certainly would want to become a butterfly soon. I'd much rather be a butterfly than a caterpillar, wouldn't you? *(Nod your head as you ask, to encourage the response.)* Is there anybody here who would like to be a creepy-crawly caterpillar, eating leaves? *(Pause only slightly.)* How about a butterfly? How many of you would rather be a butterfly? *(Raise your hand and pause for response.)*

You already are a butterfly! Each one of you, in God's eyes, looks like a beautiful butterfly, one of the most beautiful creatures on earth! *(Hold up either the butterfly or the picture of the caterpillar as you speak.)* The Bible says that Christians are new creatures; the old—caterpillar—has gone and the new—butterfly— has come.

By ourselves, we may be a lot like caterpillars; not too nice, even doing some damage. But when we believe in Jesus and are Christians, we become entirely new creatures, like this butterfly. We can't change ourselves; only God can do that. And he does that through Jesus.

You may think that all this sounds very compli- cated, but you don't have to worry about that at all. You only have to know that maybe you were a cater- pillar once, but now you're a butterfly in God's sight. Anyone who believes in Jesus is a butterfly.

The next time you see a butterfly outside, watch it and enjoy it. Think about how it was once a cater- pillar. And remember that if you love Jesus, God looks at you, forgets the caterpillar, and sees a beau- tiful butterfly.

12

Invisible Umbrellas

Scripture: You have been a refuge for the poor, a refuge for the needy in his distress, a shelter from the storm and a shade from the heat (Isa. 25:4).

Concept: God protects those who love him.

Object: An umbrella.

Song: "A Shelter in the Time of Storm," "Safe Am I."

I brought my umbrella with me today because I thought it was going to rain (*or* the sun was getting hot). An umbrella is a really good shelter, isn't it? *(Open the umbrella.)* If it's raining and you must go outside, all you do is hold this over your head. *(Demonstrate.)* That shelters you from the rain.

Or if it's too hot outside and you need a little shade, hold this over your head. *(Demonstrate.)* Then you're walking in shade wherever you go.

How many of you own an umbrella? *(Raise your hand and pause for response.)* Good. I'm glad you do. An umbrella is a good thing to have. It's a good shelter to carry with you.

How many of you have your umbrellas here with you? *(Pause for response.)* No one? Well, don't worry.

I have good news for you. Each one of you has an umbrella with you today. You can't see it, but it's right over your head.

Look up. *(Look upward and pause.)* Can you see an umbrella over you? *(Shake your head and pause for response.)* No! I can't either, but your umbrella is surely there.

Your umbrella is invisible. That means you can't see it. Air is invisible; you can't see air. But air is all around us. My words are invisible; you can't see them. But you can hear me; my words are real. Love is invisible; you can't see it. Yet your parents love you and God loves you. Love is real, but you can't see it. And so is that umbrella over you. It's invisible; you can't see it.

But that umbrella over you is as real as this umbrella *(hold up the umbrella)*, and it's much, much better than this one.

The umbrella that's over you right now is God's love. Remember I just said that love is invisible and you can't see it? That's why you can't see your umbrella; it's made of God's love. God surrounds you with his love.

God promised to be a shelter from storms and a shade from heat. That sounds like an umbrella *(hold up the umbrella)*, doesn't it? But that doesn't mean that God's love will keep you dry when it rains or will give you shade on a sunny day. God was using picture-talk in the Bible.

When God said that he would be a shelter and a shade he meant that he would always protect you.

God wants only the best for you. He doesn't want you to have a lot of trouble in your life. So, God said that if you love him, he will protect you from a lot of troubles in life. That's what he meant by shelter and shade. He'll cover you, like an umbrella, with love and protect you from troubles worse than rainstorms.

Now, that picture-talk is sometimes a little difficult to imagine, so we're going to help our imaginations a bit today. We're going to act like we have umbrellas, to help us picture our invisible umbrellas.

First, I'll give you each an invisible umbrella. *(Pass out the invisible umbrellas. Continue to speak as you distribute them.)* Take it from my hand, but don't put it up yet. Just think about the real, invisible umbrella of God's love that always covers you. This invisible umbrella I'm giving you just helps you imagine that umbrella of God's love. God's love really does cover you.

Do you all have your invisible umbrellas now? Let's open them and put them up over our heads. *(Open your invisible umbrella and hold it over your head. If the children don't respond, tell them to pretend to open their umbrellas.)* Now you are all protected. Make sure that you hold your umbrella up. *(Demonstrate and keep holding yours up.)*

We're just pretending to hold umbrellas up, to help our imaginations. These are our invisible umbrellas of God's love.

But God's love isn't pretend, is it? It will always surround you and keep you close to him. You can close your invisible umbrella now. *(Demonstrate.)*

13

God's Dandelion

Scripture: The earth is the LORD'S and everything in it, the world, and all who live in it
(Ps. 24:1).

Concept: Creation belongs to God; we should
treat it with care.

Objects: A dandelion (or any flower with lots
of petals or parts), an acorn, a pine cone, and
a roll of tape or a bottle of glue. (*Note:* You
can use other natural objects instead of an
acorn and pine cone.)

Song: "This Is My Father's World."

What kind of flower is this? *(Hold up the
dandelion. Pause for response.)* It's a dandelion, of
course. Everyone knows what a dandelion is. There
are lots of them around. I picked this one right outside of church.

Who made this dandelion? *(Pause for response.)*
God did! God made all flowers, didn't he?

I'm going to try a little experiment with God's
dandelion here. Maybe you can help. I'm going to
see if I can make a dandelion from these parts.

First, I have to pull it apart. *(Pull off the petals. Continue to speak as you do so.)* I know that these petals all

fit around this little part in the middle. They all point upward toward the sun. If I can remember how they're put on the flower, maybe I can make the dandelion, too, out of the parts.

There, all the petals are off. Now let's try making God's dandelion all over again.

(Hold up the tape or glue.) I thought I'd use this to put the flower back together again. Do you think this will work? *(Pause for response.)* No? Well, if *(whatever you have)* won't work, do you think *(the other adhesive)* will? *(Pause for response.)* No?

What can I use to put God's dandelion back together again? *(Pause for response. Repeat their responses.)* Is there anything I can use to make God's dandelion all over again? *(Pause for response.)* No? I don't think so either. Only God can make a dandelion.

If I were very, very careful, and glued (*or* taped) all the petals back on the flower, would this dandelion live? *(Pause for response.)* No! I don't know how to make a flower live. Nobody except God knows how to make a flower live. I think I've ruined God's dandelion.

(Hold up the acorn.) What's this? *(Pause for response.)* That's right, it's an acorn. There are lots of acorns around. Some of them grow into oak trees; squirrels and birds eat some of them. They're very useful.

Who made this acorn? *(Pause for response.)* God did! It's his. God made all acorns, didn't he?

If I pulled God's acorn apart, would I be able to put it back together again? *(Pause for response.)* Of course not! I ruin God's acorn when I pull it apart. It would never grow into a huge oak tree. And if I just threw it away, it would never feed squirrels or birds.

(Hold up the pine cone.) What's this? *(Pause for response.)* That's right, it's a pine cone. There are lots of pine cones around. Some drop seeds to make new pine trees; some feed squirrels and birds. Pine cones are very useful.

Who made this pine cone? *(Pause for response.)* God did! It's his. God made all pine cones, didn't he?

If I pulled God's pine cone apart, would I be able to put it back together again? *(Pause for response.)* Of course not! I ruin God's pine cone when I pull it apart. It would never grow into a pine tree. And if I just threw it away, it would never feed squirrels or birds.

(Hold up the dandelion remains, the acorn, and the pine cone.) Let's say this dandelion, acorn, and pine cone stand for all the flowers, trees, and all living things in the world. Who made them? *(Pause for response.)* You're right, God did! Who do they belong to? *(Pause for response.)* Yes, all of creation belongs to God. He made it.

(Hold up just the dandelion remains.) If we pull pieces of creation apart, can we put them back together again? *(Pause for response.)* Of course not! Only God can make living dandelions. Only God can make acorns grow into oak trees and pine cones grow into pine trees.

So, do you think we should tear all of God's dandelions apart, or should we be careful with them? *(Pause for response.)* Of course, we should be very careful. Creation belongs to God, and we should treat it with care.

(Hold up the acorn and the pine cone.) But squirrels and birds eat some of these things. Others grow into oak trees and pine trees. May we use some of God's

creation? *(Nod, and pause for response.)* Of course! God gave us some plants for food. He gave us ways to make our homes and ways to make clothes, all from his creation. God told us that we may use creation.

(Hold up the dandelion remains.) But we should use it wisely. We shouldn't just pull it apart, like this. God also told us to care for his creation. He gave us a wonderful world to enjoy and to care for.

When you leave church this morning (*or* when you go home) you may see lots of dandelions (*or* acorns, *or* pine cones). You may even want to pick (*or* pick up) one to keep as a reminder this week. But don't waste them. Use creation—even God's dandelions—carefully. They all belong to God; we should treat them with care.

Try It, You'll Like It!

Scripture: Taste and see that the LORD is good (Ps. 34:8).

Concept: We each need a personal relationship with God.

Objects: A few unfamiliar fruits. (*Note:* If no unfamiliar fruits are available, you can use cans of unfamiliar foods. Simply substitute the food names for the fruits used here.)

I found some special fruits at the store this week. I wonder if any of you know what these are.

(Show the star fruit.) This is a star fruit. Has anyone here eaten star fruit? *(Pause slightly.)* I thought probably no one here had eaten it. It's not a common fruit. Is star fruit good? *(Pause just a second.)* You don't know, do you? How can you tell if star fruit is good until you've tasted it? You have to taste it for yourself before you really know if it tastes good.

(Show the pomegranate.) This is a pomegranate. Is a pomegranate good? *(Pause slightly.)* You don't know, do you? That's because you've never tasted it. What must you do to know if a pomegranate is good? *(Pause for response.)* Yes, you must taste it for yourself. I could tell you that it's good, but you might

not like exactly what I like. You must taste the fruit for yourself.

(Show the guava.) This is a guava. Is a guava good? *(Pause slightly.)* You don't know, do you? You've never tasted a guava. If I tell you it's good, will you believe me? *(Shake your head and pause slightly.)* Not exactly. What must you do to know if a guava is good? *(Pause for response.)* Yes, you must taste it for yourself!

Do you ever get strange food at home? Maybe someone cooks a food that you have never eaten before, and you're not sure you'll like it. What do your mom and dad usually say to you? *(Pause for response.)* They probably say something like, "Try it, you'll like it" or "You won't know if you like it unless you try it." You must taste it for yourself to know if it's good.

The Bible says that about God! It says, "Taste and see that the Lord is good." In other words, you have to try God for yourself to see if he is as good as we say.

How can you try God for yourself? *(Pause for response. You may have to lead them with a few questions.)* Can you pray, all by yourself? Can you talk to Jesus alone, just you and Jesus? Can you read Bible stories yourself, or have someone read them just to you? Can you think about God all by yourself?

You can do all those things! If you can read, sit down and read some Bible stories all by yourself. Or ask someone to read a Bible story to you alone. That's like God talking just to you, not to you through a teacher.

And after those stories, you can think about them all by yourself. Sometimes we talk about them and share what we think. But it's good to think your own thoughts about the stories, too.

You can pray all by yourself, too, just you with your own words. "Jesus, this is Ryan *(the name of a child in your audience)* speaking. This is just me saying my own words." That's a conversation between you and Jesus alone.

You can do all these things to try God for yourself. That's what the Bible calls tasting the Lord. You must taste for yourself to see how good God is. And you'll find that God is very, very good.

(Show them the fruits.) Someday you may be able to try these. I think they're good, but you must taste them for yourself. Maybe this week you'll come across a new food that's strange to you. To find out if you like it, what must you do? *(Pause for response.)* Yes, you must taste it yourself! As you do you can remember that you also must "taste" God yourself. Listen to those Bible stories and pray all by yourself. Taste and see that the Lord is good!

15

A Longer-than-Lifetime Guarantee

Scripture: God has said, "Never will I leave you; never will I forsake you" (Heb. 13:5).

Concept: God will always be with us.

Objects: A few written guarantees from household objects.

Song: "No, Never Alone."

I wanted to bring along my TV, my VCR, and my telephone today, but that was a little too much to carry. So I brought these little guarantees that came with them instead. We'll just imagine that we have the TV, VCR, and telephone here.

(Show them one guarantee.) This came with the TV. It says on the back that the TV is guaranteed to work for two years. If something goes wrong within two years, I can take it back. That's what a guarantee means. But after two years, it's not guaranteed. If it breaks down, I'll have to get a new one.

Do you think that the TV will break down some day? *(Pause for response.)* Yes, it sure will! TVs don't last forever. It will probably last at least two years, but eventually it will break down. I'll have to get rid of it and get another.

(Show them another guarantee.) This came with my VCR. It's also a two-year guarantee. So how long do you think my VCR will last? *(Pause for response.)* Probably a little longer than two years. VCRs break down, too. Someday my VCR won't work, and I'll have to get another.

(Show them another guarantee.) This came with my telephone. It guarantees the phone for only one year. Is my phone going to stop working someday? *(Pause for response.)* Yes! It's guaranteed to work, but only for a year. After that, it will probably break down, like just about everything else.

Everything that you buy breaks down sooner or later. *(Show the guarantees.)* Most things are guaranteed to work for a while, but they're not guaranteed to work forever. Nothing in this world lasts forever.

Even friends don't last forever, do they? Friends don't come with written guarantees *(show the guarantees)* for so many years. Sometimes friends move away, and you can't play with them anymore. Or you move away and must make new friends. Has anyone here ever lost a friend? *(Raise your hand as you ask the question to encourage a like response.)* Then you know that it hurts to lose friends. But you can find new friends; old friends don't last forever.

Option

(Consider your audience carefully before you decide to include or skip this next paragraph.)

Sometimes families don't last forever, do they? Even families don't come with guarantees. Sometimes a parent dies or a parent leaves the family, and that really hurts. Sometimes a new parent can ease the hurt, but you still know that families don't last forever. Nothing lasts forever. Nothing comes with forever guarantees, does it?

Continue Lesson

Wait a minute! I can think of one person who lasts forever. Who is that? *(Pause for response.)* Yes! God *(or Jesus)* is forever. He will never, ever die.

And do you know what? God has given us a written guarantee *(show the guarantees)* like these only much, much better. It's a longer-than-lifetime guarantee, written in the Bible.

God says in the Bible, "Never will I leave you; never will I forsake you." God has promised to be your parent. He'll be a parent forever. God will never leave you. No matter where you move, he'll be there, a friend forever. He will never walk out on you. He will never fail you. He will always be with you—forever. That's a longer-than-lifetime guarantee.

So, if you're missing a friend or a part of your family, it's OK to be sad. That's normal. But that can also help you remember that God will never leave you; he will always be nearby.

The next time you have trouble with a toy, or the TV or VCR, or the phone, ask someone to check the guarantee. *(Show the guarantees.)* It might have run out. Remember God's guarantee in the Bible; it never runs out. God will never leave you. He will always be near.

16

Counting Cares or Hairs

Scripture: Indeed, the very hairs of your head are all numbered. Don't be afraid (Luke 12:7).

Concept: God cares for you.

Object: None.

I didn't bring anything to show you today. You brought it! That's right, you came right down here with just what I want to talk about—your hair!

Everybody here has hair on their head, don't they? And everybody's hair is just a little different from everybody else's hair.

Run your fingers through your own hair. *(Demonstrate.)* There's lots of it, isn't there? It's all over your head. Even if it's short, there's still lots of it.

Let's try to count some of our hairs. Each of you can count your own. It's going to be sort of hard to do, but try it. Take a little bit of hair and roll it between your fingers, like this. *(Demonstrate.)* While you're rolling it, count. We can't feel each hair, so we'll just have to guess, like this: one, two, three, four . . . *(up to ten. Demonstrate as you count, with just a little bit of hair.)* Then try another spot, and do it again. *(Move to a different part of your scalp.)* Then another spot. *(Count up to ten slowly on each spot, encouraging the children to follow suit. Stop when they begin to lose interest.)*

There, that's enough to make my point. Do you think you can count all the hairs on your head? *(Pause for response.)* No! There are way too many hairs on your head to count.

It really doesn't matter, does it? Who cares exactly how many hairs they have? So what if Sara has a hundred more hairs than Jeff? It doesn't matter at all, does it? *(Shake your head for emphasis.)*

Yet, somebody has counted the hairs on your head. Somebody knows exactly how many hairs you and you and you *(point to individual children and name them if you can)* have on your head. Somebody knows those big numbers. Who is that? *(Pause for response.)* That's right, God! Jesus said that the hairs of your head are all numbered. He knows exactly how many hairs you have. He can count that high, and he has.

Why does God want to know how many hairs you have on your head? *(Pause for response.)* Because he cares about you! When you love someone, when you really care about them, you want to know all about them. God loves you so much that he wants to know all about you. He cares so much that he knows how many hairs you have on your head!

If God is great enough to count the hairs on your head, and if he cares enough about you to really count them, is he going to take care of you? *(Pause for response.)* Of course. After Jesus said that the hairs of your head are numbered, he added, "Don't be afraid." God, who can do anything, knows all about you, loves you, and has promised to take care of you.

That's a wonderful thing to think about the next time you comb your hair. Look in the mirror and try to count a few strands. Then you can remember that God loves you enough to know exactly how many hairs you have. And he has told you that he will take care of you.

17

Sweeter than Honey

Scripture: How sweet are your words to my taste, sweeter than honey to my mouth! (Ps. 119:103).

Concept: God promises us good things.

Object: A jar of honey.

What's this? *(Hold up the jar. Pause for response.)* Yes, it's a jar of honey! How many of you like honey? *(Pause for response.)* I do, too. Almost everybody likes honey.

Is honey sweet or sour? *(Pause for response.)* Of course, it's sweet. It's probably one of the sweetest things there is. Can you think of anything that's sweeter than honey? *(Pause for response and discuss their responses.)* Sugar? Some people think so, but some people prefer honey. Maybe sugar is sweeter, maybe not. Jelly? Jelly's sweet all right, but it tastes different from honey. It's difficult to tell which is sweeter. *(Continue until you run out of suggestions.)*

Honey certainly is one of the sweetest things there is. But I know of something sweeter than honey: God's words. The Bible says that God's words are sweeter than honey to our mouths.

That sounds strange, doesn't it? We don't really taste God's words, do we? How can they be sweet?

Well, the Bible is using picture language here, just like we do sometimes. Here's some of our picture language. "That's such a *sweet* baby." "How *sweet* of you to do that." "What a *sweet* vacation we had." "That's *sweet.*" Sometimes, to mean really, really good or really, really nice we say *sweet*. You're a bunch of *sweet* kids. You know what that means, don't you?

That's what the Bible means when it says that God's words are sweeter than honey. It means that God's words are really, really good. We think they're better, even, than honey!

What are some of God's words? What does God say to us? *(Pause for response. You may have to prompt them with some questions.)* Does God say that he will take care of us always? Does God say that he will always love us? Does God say that he will never forsake, or leave, us? And best of all, does God say that we can live with him if we believe in Jesus? Are these really, really good words? *(Pause for response.)* Yes, they're *sweet*. In fact, they're sweeter than *(hold up the jar)* honey!

So, the next time you see a jar of honey, or you eat some honey, think of how sweet it is. Try to think of something sweeter than honey. That will remind you of God's words to you.

What's sweeter than honey? *(Pause for response.)* That's right; God's words are sweeter than honey.

18

Acting Like Ants

Scripture: Go to the ant, you sluggard; consider its ways and be wise! (Prov. 6:6).

Nobody should seek his own good, but the good of others (1 Cor. 10:24).

Concept: We should cooperate with each other.

Object: Ants in a jar.

Who can tell me what these are? *(Show the jar and pause for response.)* That's right, they're ants. I picked them up near an anthill yesterday.

Watch them for a little while. *(Hold up the jar so all can see.)* What are they doing? *(Pause for response.)* Not much, that's right. They're just walking around. That's about all they can do in a jar. I think that they want to get out and go back home, to their anthill, where they belong.

It's fun to watch ants working together at their anthill. If you watch for a while, you can see them following each other to food, taking food home, cleaning out the anthill, or building the anthill. Sometimes you can see them trying to protect their anthill.

The nice thing is that they always work together, cooperate, to get the job done. God made them to work that way. You can see them cooperate, if you watch them right at the anthill.

And if you watch ants work at their anthill, you're doing what the Bible tells us to do. The Bible says, "Go to the ant . . . consider its ways." That's a surprise, isn't it? Why watch ants? Well, the Bible goes on to say, "Consider its ways and be wise." Maybe we can learn something from watching ants.

What do the ants do at their anthill? *(Pause for response. You may have to lead them with a few questions.)* They work? Do they work alone or together? Do they fight with each other or cooperate? That's right! They all work together. They cooperate.

Maybe that's what God wants us to see. The Bible talks about how ants store food. They do this by working together. So maybe the Bible is saying something like, "Go and watch ants. See how well they cooperate to get things done at home."

Do you think God wants us to cooperate at home? *(Pause for response.)* Of course! We should cooperate like the ants.

In what ways can you cooperate at home? *(Pause for response. You may or may not have to use the next questions.)* Can you pick up your toys when asked? Can you share toys? Can you help with a younger brother or sister? Can you go to bed nicely when asked? Can you say your prayers nicely at the table?

You can probably think of many ways to cooperate at home. And because you're a person and not just an ant, you can be sweet and loving while you cooperate. You can work together at home because you love your family and they love you. Ants cooperate, but they can't love.

I brought these ants in a jar *(hold up the jar)* just to help you picture ants near their home. I'll put these back near the anthill after the service. If you see any ants this week, take some time to watch them. You'll see them work together, and that can remind you of how to cooperate at home.

19

News from God

Scripture: But these are written that you may believe that Jesus is the Christ, the Son of God, and that by believing you may have life in his name (John 20:31).

Concept: The Bible tells us the world's most important news: Jesus saves.

Objects: A newspaper (it should be a few days old), a Bible. (*Note:* This lesson can be done with Christmas cards. The concept then is that the Bible tells us that Jesus was born. Links to Christmas cards are (1) They're to a certain person [Rom. 1:16]; (2) They're from a certain person [2 Tim. 3:16]; and (3) They celebrate Christmas [the Christmas story and Matt. 16:16].)

Song: "The B-I-B-L-E," "I Have a Wonderful Treasure."

Who can tell me what this is? *(Hold up the newspaper and pause for response.)* That's right, it's a newspaper. This is the (name of the paper). I (*or* some people) read it every day to get the latest news. I like to know the news of the world.

This paper was printed (<u>the date</u>). It's a bit old now; the news is stale and out of date. That's the trouble with newspapers: After a day, they're out of date. The news isn't news anymore, the paper isn't worth a thing, and it goes on the recycle pile. I must read a newspaper every day to keep up-to-date on important world news.

I keep reading the newspaper because it's important to know world news. I should know if a storm is coming, or if prices are going up. Suppose I read about a lot of people starving in a certain country. Maybe I could send food or money. Or I might read about a big earthquake someplace; I could send clothes or maybe go there and help. I must know the news of the world, and the newspaper tells me all I have to know.

Well, not quite all. There's another "newspaper" that tells me all I have to know. It's not really a newspaper, it's a book. But it does tell me the most important news in the world. What book am I talking about? *(Hold up the Bible as you ask the question and pause for response.)* That's right, the Bible!

The Bible tells us the most important news in the whole wide world, that Jesus saves us from our sins. It also tells us stories; it tells us how and where Jesus was born, and how and where Jesus died to save us, and lots of other stories. And it tells us how to live—to love Jesus and to love each other. The Bible is our best "newspaper," giving us the best news in the world.

And that news never goes out of date! The Bible was written a long time ago, but it still tells us about Jesus, and Jesus is still the most important news in the world. We never have to throw our Bibles on the recycle pile, do we? *(Shake your head and pause for response.)* No! The Bible is always up-to-date with the most important news in the world. *(Hold up the Bible as you speak and keep it up.)*

(Hold up the newspaper, next to the Bible.) How many of you get newspapers at your house? *(Pause for response.)* I think most people do. When you see an adult reading the newspaper at your house this week, remember the other "newspaper," the one that tells us about Jesus. What's that other "newspaper" called? *(Indicate the Bible and pause for response.)* Yes, the Bible.

When you see a stack of newspapers in the recycle pile this week you can say, "God's newspaper is never out of date. Jesus is always the world's most important news."

Flowers Don't Worry

Scripture: Consider how the lilies grow. They do not labor or spin. Yet I tell you, not even Solomon in all his splendor was dressed like one of these. If that is how God clothes the grass of the field, . . . how much more will he clothe you, O you of little faith! And do not set your heart on what you will eat or drink; do not worry about it. . . . Your Father knows that you need them (Luke 12:27–30).

Concept: God will take care of you.

Object: A bouquet of wildflowers. (It would be nice, but not necessary, to have one flower for each child.)

$\mathbf{S}$ee the pretty flowers I picked yesterday? *(Hold the bouquet up for all to see.)* They were growing in a field near my house *(or wherever you got them).* They're beautiful, aren't they?

(Continue to hold up the bouquet and point out different flowers as you talk about them.)

I especially like all the different colors *(or all the beautiful yellows or reds or whatever).* They are so brilliant, they catch your attention immediately. Wouldn't you love to be dressed in colors like that?

And how about all these sizes? Some are so tiny, they barely look like flowers until they're clustered together. Others are so big you can't miss them. And some are just the right size to hold big bumblebees that visit them. Could you think up all these sizes if you made flowers? I know I couldn't.

The shapes are fun, too. Some are round and flat, easy to see. Others have lots of ruffled petals, and others seem to have no shape at all until you really look at them. When you look closely, you can see some amazing shapes in these flowers.

(Continue in this manner until you feel that you've made the point: These flowers are wonderful, gorgeous creations.)

You know what's special about these flowers? They don't even think about how beautiful they are—flowers can't think—they just grow. And they automatically grow just like this. Well, not quite automatically.

Who made each of these wildflowers? *(Pause for response.)* God did, of course! Only God can make these living flowers. It seems to me that God took special care to make such beautiful flowers.

Jesus once talked about beautiful wildflowers. He told us to look at how they grow. That's what we just did. We looked at the flowers and said that God must have taken special care to make them.

But Jesus didn't stop there. He said that we should see how beautiful God made the flowers and how he takes care of them. Then we should know that God will take even better care of us.

Jesus said that we don't have to worry about what we will eat or drink because God knows what we need, and he will give us exactly what we need.

Just like these flowers *(indicate the bouquet)* don't think about what they need, so we shouldn't either. God loves us much more than flowers, and he'll care for us even better than he cares for flowers.

So I think this bouquet and all wildflowers are really special. They can remind us of God's love and care. When we see these beautiful flowers growing just right, we can remember what Jesus said, God cares for them, but he cares much more for us.

Option

(Add the following paragraph if you have flowers for the children.)

I've got some flowers for you to take home. Be sure to care for them. Put them in some water so they will live for a while. And when you look at them, remember that God cares for you.

Powerful Punch

Scripture: You are the salt of the earth (Matt. 5:13).

But love your enemies, do good to them, and lend to them without expecting to get anything back (Luke 6:35).

Concept: Jesus wants us to flavor the world with love.

Objects: A glass of water, a spoon, some drink (punch, iced tea, a dark Kool Aid) mix.

I want to make some punch. I have everything here *(show them the glass of water, the spoon, and the punch mix)*, but I'm not quite sure what to do. Can you help me?

(Show them the glass of water.) I have the water here *(take one swallow)*, but it doesn't taste like punch. I haven't done anything to it yet. It tastes like water.

What do I need to make this taste like punch? *(Pause for response.)* Yes, I need the punch! *(Hold up the punch mix, dip a finger into it, and take a little taste.)* That's punch all right, I can sure taste that.

(Hold up the glass.) Now that I have both, do I have punch? *(Pause for response.)* No. My water hasn't changed, has it? It's still just plain water. What must

I do to make punch? *(Pause for response.)* Of course, I must stir this punch mix into the water.

(Mix just a little punch into the water and taste the drink.) There, now I'm getting my punch. The water didn't taste like punch until I stirred the punch mix into it. I flavored the water with punch mix and got punch.

This *(hold up the glass and the punch mix)* reminds me of something Jesus wants us to do. Jesus wants us to flavor the world for him. Jesus wants us to be kind and loving to people so that people can feel love and kindness.

(Hold up the glass.) Here we have people who need love and kindness. It doesn't look like there's much here yet, does it?

(Hold up the drink mix.) Here we have Christians like you and me. We try to be kind and loving, don't we? Jesus told us that we should, and he helps us to be good and kind and loving.

(Hold up the glass and the crystals together, indicating which you are talking about.) Of course we try to be good and kind and loving to each other. That's rather like this punch mix in its jar. It's fine where it is, but it isn't doing anything in the water. If we're good and kind and loving only to each other, we're not really flavoring the world for Jesus.

How can we flavor the world with goodness, kindness, and love, like Jesus wants us to? *(Pause for response.)* That's right, we can be good and kind and loving to everyone. That will help flavor the world for Jesus.

Every time we share some of our things *(put a little punch mix into the water)*, every time we are helpful and pleasant *(put a little more punch mix into the water)*, every time we show love *(put some more punch into the water)* to our neighbors and to everyone, we are flavoring the world for Jesus. The more we love people and do good, the more we flavor the world for Jesus. *(Hold up the glass of now dark punch.)*

Maybe you don't like powerful punch too much. But we can also make loving lemonade or tasty tea the same way. There are lots of drinks that you make by stirring mix into water, just like there are lots of ways you can flavor the world for Jesus.

Option 1

(The following paragraphs will work if some of the children are school age and above.)

So, I'd like you to try a little experiment this week. Some adult should help you with it. When you return from church this morning, see how many different drink mixes you have on your shelf. There's probably coffee, punch, chocolate, lemonade, Kool-Aid, and maybe a few more. Take them all out and line them up where you can see them. They can remind you to flavor the world for Jesus.

Try to think of ways you can flavor the world. Maybe you can share a toy. Maybe you can be especially nice to a neighbor. Maybe you can tell someone that Jesus loves them. Ask an adult to help you think of ways.

When you think of a way to flavor the world, try to do that. Go out and share a toy with a neighbor. After you do, put one of those drink mixes back into the cupboard or ask an adult to put it back for you.

80

Then tell someone that Jesus loves them. Put another drink mix back into the cupboard. Try to get all those mixes back on the shelf by using them as reminders to flavor the world for Jesus.

Option 2

(If the children are very young, use the following paragraph.)

Sometime this week you'll probably get thirsty and ask for a glass of punch or juice or lemonade. When you do, look at the punch before you drink it. Somebody put flavor into it so that it would be good to drink. That can remind you that you, too, should flavor the world for Jesus.

T-Shirt Christians

Scripture: . . . that they may see your good deeds and praise your Father in heaven (Matt. 5:16).

Concept: Our actions should bring praise to God.

Object: A T-shirt with a message or advertisement printed on it.

I brought a T-shirt with me today. *(Hold up the T-shirt so the children can see the printing.)* It says, (the message on the shirt). Apparently, whoever wears this shirt wants people to think about (the product or the message).

If I had a T-shirt that said "flowers" in big letters and had pictures of flowers on it, what would you think about when you saw the shirt? *(Pause for response.)* Of course, you'd think about flowers.

Or if a T-shirt said "I love robins" and had pictures of robins on it, what would you think about when you saw it? *(Pause for response.)* That's right, robins.

(Hold up the shirt again.) What do you think about when you see this shirt? *(Pause for response.)* Yes, (the product or the message)!

I see lots of T-shirts with messages on them, don't you? *(Nod your head and pause for response.)* I guess lots of people want us to think about certain things, so they wear a T-shirt to tell about that thing. Then everybody who sees the T-shirt thinks about whatever it tells about.

Jesus once said that we should be like T-shirts. Well, he didn't really say, "You should be like T-shirts," but he did say that people should look at us and think of God. He said that people should "see your good deeds and praise your Father in heaven."

That's just like being a T-shirt. *(Hold up the shirt.)* People look at this and think of (<u>the product or the message</u>); they should look at you and praise God.

How can you make people think about God and praise him when they see you? Here's a hint: God is love. God told us to love one another and love him. Should you be kind and loving to people? *(Pause for response.)* Yes, I think so. That's what God told us to do.

How can you be kind and loving to people? *(Pause for response. You may have to prompt them with a few questions.)* Can you share your toys? Can you smile and speak nicely to people? Can you help a friend with chores? Can you obey your parents cheerfully? There are all sorts of ways you can be kind and loving to people.

When you do those things—when you're kind and loving to people—you're just like a T-shirt. *(Hold up the T-shirt.)* People see you and praise God for love.

You don't need a T-shirt *(hold up the T-shirt)* to tell about God, do you? Your actions can bring praise to God. But the next time you see a T-shirt like this one with a message on it, look at the shirt and think of the message. That will remind you that people should look at you and praise God.

Argument with a Fly

Scripture: Don't have anything to do with foolish and stupid arguments, because you know
they produce quarrels. And the Lord's ser-
vant must not quarrel; instead, he must be
kind to everyone, able to teach, not resentful
(2 Tim. 2:23–24).

Concept: We should avoid foolish and stupid
arguments.

Object: A housefly in a jar.

I caught this fly in my house yesterday.
(Hold up the jar.) I was going to put it outside but
decided to show it to you first.

This fly belongs outside, doesn't it? No one wants
houseflies in their house. They don't belong there,
and they're not good for us.

We especially don't want flies to sit on our food,
do we? Houseflies carry lots of germs that aren't good
for us. What happens when they sit on our food?
*(Pause for response. You may have to prompt them with
a few questions.)* Do they leave germs on our food?
Can those germs make us sick? Yes, they do, sometimes. When flies sit on our food they spread germs

that can make us sick. So we shoo them off the food right away.

In fact, we don't really like to have flies near us, do we? They can spread germs when we handle them or if they land on us. The germs they carry seem to be OK for them, but not for us. So we simply stay away from flies.

When you see houseflies outside, do you run up to them and try to get them to sit on you? *(Shake your head as you ask the question and pause for response.)* Of course not. You stay away from houseflies. And when they sit on your food, even at a picnic, what do you do? *(Motion as if to shoo away a fly and pause for response.)* That's right, you shoo them away.

Do you run up to wasps and bees if you see them outside? *(Pause for response.)* No! They're OK outside where they belong. Yet we still stay away from them because wasps, bees, and people don't mix well. Wasps and bees sting if we bother them.

If a bee or wasp mistakes you for a flower and sits on you, do you usually just let it sit? *(Pause for response.)* Usually not. Most people gently brush them off, because those little things can sting.

There are some things that you simply stay away from, or that you shoo away if they come too close to you.

In the Bible, God tells us that there are some things that we should simply "avoid"—or stay away from. God doesn't talk about shooing away flies, but the Bible does mention other things we should avoid.

One of the things we should avoid is silly arguments. In fact, the Bible calls them "foolish and stupid arguments."

Let me show you a foolish and stupid argument. *(Use a very peevish voice and irritated face. Much of the success of the lesson depends on how realistic, yet overdone, you can make the arguments sound.)* "Did too!" "Did not!" "Did too!" "Did not!" "Did too!" "Did not!"

Have you ever argued like that with someone? *(Pause for response.)* Yes, we probably all have. But it doesn't get you anywhere, does it? It's a foolish and stupid argument.

How about this: "This is mine." "No, it's mine." "Mine." "Mine." "Mine!" "Mine!" Is this a foolish and stupid argument? *(Nod your head.)* Yes, it is. Yet we all argue like that sometimes. God tells us to avoid that foolish argument.

Here's one more: "Mom, he hit me!" "She did it first!" "He did it first!" "She did it first!" "He did it first!" "She did it first!" Is this a foolish and stupid argument? *(Nod your head.)* Yes, it is. Should we avoid foolish and stupid arguments? *(Pause for response.)* Yes, God tells us to avoid them.

If you hear someone starting an argument, walk away. Don't argue. Avoid foolish and stupid arguments *(hold up the jar)* just like you avoid germy flies.

In fact, God says that we should be kind to everyone. So if someone starts arguing with you, answer with a kind word instead of an argument. *(Hold up the jar and keep it up.)* That's like shooing a fly away from you.

Next time you see a housefly inside, put it outside. And avoid those flies that are outside already. Look at them and think that they're just like foolish and stupid arguments.

If you hear a foolish and stupid argument starting, stay away from it too or shoo it off with kindness. It's just like a housefly. It's one of those things in life we should avoid.

No Busy Signals

Scripture: The LORD . . . hears the prayer of the righteous (Prov. 15:29).

Concept: God always hears our prayers.

Object: A telephone.

Song: "Hear Our Prayer, O Lord."

I tried to call a friend of mine shortly before I left this morning, but the line was busy. *(Show them the phone.)* All I got was a busy signal. So I decided to take this along and try again.

I wouldn't really make a phone call during our service, but we can pretend. *(Pretend to dial the number and listen for a minute.)* Now I got his (her) answering machine. I don't want to talk to a machine, I want to talk to my friend. But I can't seem to get through. Either the line is busy or I get his (her) machine. That seems to happen often lately; I call a certain person but can't talk to him (her).

How many of you have talked on your telephone? *(Raise your hand and pause for response.)* How many of you have tried to call a friend and gotten a busy signal or an answering machine? *(Pause for response.)* Then you know how frustrating that can be. If you haven't used the phone yourself, how many of you have watched an adult try and try to call someone and never get through? *(Pause for response.)* Adults can get mighty upset about that, too.

I know one person you can call who is always free—no busy signals, no machines; every time you call you can actually talk to that person. Can anybody guess who that is? *(Pause for response. Repeat their responses. If the answer isn't forthcoming, prompt them with the next question.)* Is God (*or* Jesus) ever too busy to listen to you? No! Every time you call on God, he's there to listen.

And you don't even need a telephone, do you? How can you talk to God? *(Pause for response.)* That's right, you can talk to God through prayer.

When you talk to a friend on a telephone, what do you talk about? *(Pause for response.)* You talk about all sorts of things, don't you? Sometimes you ask questions, sometimes you tell your friend some news, sometimes you just visit.

When you talk to God in prayer, what do you talk about? *(Pause for response.)* You can talk about anything that's on your mind, can't you? You can ask for help with problems, you can talk about things that are happening to you, you can tell God that you love him. God loves to have you talk to him. *(Hold up the phone and keep it up to the end of the lesson.)* He's waiting for your call.

Do you know what's really great? When you call on God—when you pray to him—you'll never get a busy signal or an answering machine. You'll always get through to God, because he always hears our prayers.

Light Your Candle

Scripture: In the same way, let your light shine before men, that they may see your good deeds and praise your Father in heaven (Matt. 5:16).

Concept: We must put some effort into letting our lights shine.

Objects: Two similar candles in candleholders, some matches.

Song: "This Little Light of Mine" or "Jesus Bids Us Shine."

I brought along some candles today. *(Hold up the candles.)* I'd like you to look at them very closely. Do these candles look like they're quite a bit the same? *(Pause for response.)* Yes, there's not much difference between the two.

Now, I'd like you to close your eyes very tightly for a minute. I'm going to get a little surprise ready for you. I'll tell you when to open your eyes.

(When their eyes are closed, light one candle. Hold both candles up again.) OK, you may open your eyes. Look at that; I lit a candle!

Which candle do you notice? *(Pause for response.)* Of course. You see the candle that's lit right away.

It's nice and bright. It almost seems to be saying, "Look at me!" Candles are meant to burn brightly, and you notice them right away when they're lit.

I'm going to blow this out now, because I don't want any accidents. *(Blow the candle out.)* I just wanted you to see how you notice a candle right away when it's burning brightly.

Only adults light candles, right? It's dangerous for kids to use matches, so let the adults in your house light any candles you have. Kids really shouldn't light candles.

Wait a minute! There is one candle you can light. In fact, there's a candle that only you can light, and you should light it. That's yourself.

That sounds strange, doesn't it? You're not a candle; you're a person. Yet Jesus compared us all to candles, and he said that we should let our lights shine.

Let me explain that a little bit. *(Hold up the candles.)* Pretend that these are people. Do you see any difference? *(Pause for response.)* No! They're just candle-people. Lots of people are like this. They don't stand out in a crowd. They look *and they act* like everyone else.

Jesus wants us to light our candles. He wants us to stand out in a crowd. He told us to let our lights shine.

(Put the candles down and light one as you speak.) Jesus said that we should let our lights shine by doing good deeds. *(Hold up the lit candle carefully and keep it up.)* Then everyone will see our good deeds and praise God.

Can anyone tell me some good deeds that would light your candle? *(Pause for response. You may have to guide them with a few questions.)* Can you be friendly?

Can you be kind? Can you share your toys? Can you show love to everyone?

(Blow on the candle just a bit.) It's not always easy to be friendly or kind, is it? Some people just aren't friendly back to you. That's kind of like this candle almost going out. Sometimes it takes a little work to keep it lit. Sometimes we have to really try hard to show love and kindness. That's letting our light shine.

I'm going to blow this candle out for good. *(Blow out the candle.)* There! It's almost easier to blow it out than to light it.

It takes a little effort, or work, to light our candles and to let our lights shine, but Jesus said that we should so people can see our good deeds and praise God. That's the way we can stand out in a crowd for him.

When you get home, I'd like you to look around the house for candles. You probably have some sitting right out in plain view. You probably haven't noticed them, because they weren't lit. They didn't stand out.

Don't light those candles. Just try to find them. Every time you see one, think about how you can light the candle of yourself. Think about the good things you can do to let your light shine for Jesus.

The Good Book

Scripture: All Scripture is God-breathed and is useful for teaching, rebuking, correcting and training in righteousness, so that the man of God may be thoroughly equipped for every good work (2 Tim. 3:16–17).

Concept: The Bible is the most important book ever written.

Objects: A novel, a textbook, a how-to book, and a Bible. (Put the books in a stack on the floor where the children can see them.)

Song: "The B-I-B-L-E."

Cleaning out my bookcase this week gave me the idea to talk to you about *(point to the books)* books!

How many of you can read? *(Raise your hand as you ask the question to encourage a like response.)* Great! Reading is fun, isn't it?

Do you like to have someone read to you? *(Nod your head as you ask, to encourage responses.)* If you can't read yet, you can enjoy someone else's reading; and you'll learn to read soon.

Since all of you will be readers soon, let's talk about good books. Here are some of the books I've read lately. *(Hold up the novel.)* This was a really good story. It was make-believe, but my imagination had a good time. I'm not sure I'll read it again, because there are lots more books like this that I haven't read.

(Hold up the textbook.) This is a good book. It isn't a story, but it gives lots of information. I wanted to know a little bit about (<u>the subject</u>), so I read this. I'm not sure I'll use it again. I'm not that interested in (<u>the subject</u>) anymore, and I know what this book had to teach about it.

(Hold up the how-to book.) This is a good book if you want to (<u>subject of the book</u>). Last year I wanted to (<u>subject of the book</u>), so I bought this book. It told me how to do it, step by step. I don't know if I'll ever (<u>subject of the book</u>) again. This is a good book, but maybe I'll give it away.

Let's see; are there any more good books around here? Can you think of any? *(Pause for response.)* What good book haven't I shown you? What's the best book there is? That's right, the Bible! *(Hold up the Bible.)*

Who gave us the Bible? *(Pause for response.)* God did, didn't he? Different people wrote different parts, but God told them what to write. That's why we say that the Bible is the Word of God.

What is the Bible about? *(Pause for response. Repeat each response. You may have to lead them with some questions.)* Is the Bible about Jesus? Does it talk about the Israelites? Does it tell us how to live? Does it tell us how to live forever? Yes, to all of those questions!

The Bible has stories in it, more stories than this book has *(hold up the novel)*. The Bible has information in it *(hold up the textbook)*, more information than this book has. And the Bible tells us how to do things *(hold up the how-to book)*, much more important things than this book does.

In the Bible God tells us how he saves us from our sins and also how we should live. Those are the most important things we will ever have to know.

(Indicate the stack of books.) I probably won't read most of these books again; I'm finished with them. *(Hold up the Bible.)* But I'll never be finished with this. The Bible is the most important book ever written.

The next time you go to the library or look through your bookcase at home, you'll see lots of big, important-looking books. They can remind you of the most important book in your life. What's that? *(Pause for response.)* The Bible. Will you ever be finished with the Bible? *(Shake your head as you ask the question and pause for response.)* No! You can read the Bible again and again and again, because the Bible, God's Word, is the most important book you'll ever read.

Who Made It?

Scripture: Through him all things were made; without him nothing was made that has been made (John 1:3).

Concept: God made all things (they didn't just happen).

Objects: Several natural objects. (What you use is irrelevant as long as they are natural objects.)

Song: "All Things Bright and Beautiful."

I went for a walk last week and picked up several natural things to show you.

(Show them a flower.) I think this flower is really pretty, don't you? *(Pause for response.)* I found it growing in a field. Who made this flower? *(Pause for response.)* Of course, God did! Can any of us make a flower? *(Pause for response.)* No! Only God can make a beautiful, living flower.

(Show them the leaves.) These were growing on a nearby tree. Leaves help trees breathe. I don't know how, but they do. Who made these leaves? *(Pause for response.)* God did! Only God can make leaves like these.

(Show them a spider in a jar.) I caught this spider very carefully and will let it go after the service. I

think it's amazing the way spiders make such complicated webs. Who made this spider? *(Pause for response.)* God did! Only God can make such wonderful, living spiders.

(Show them a rock.) This rock isn't living, but it's still pretty great. Look at all the colors in it. This is a heavy, solid rock. Who made this rock? *(Pause for response.)* God did. Can any of us make a rock? *(Pause for response.)* Of course not; only God can make a rock like this.

(Note: The idea is to show a natural object, comment about it, and ask who made it. The children should feel the rhythm of looking at something and saying, "God made it." Four or five objects should be plenty. If you don't have enough objects, continue by naming things, e.g. trees, birds, bunnies, fish, lakes, etc. Continue in this manner until you think the children have become excited. Their response can alert you: "God did" will increase in volume. Then move on to the following paragraphs.)

Who made the whole world and everything in it? *(Pause for response.)* You're right, God did. The very first words of the Bible talk about God creating the world and all life. Again and again the Bible tells us that God made all things. We know that God made the whole world and everything in it. Some people aren't quite sure. They think that the world just happened. But the Bible tells us that God made it.

So, when you see a rock *(show them the rock)* you can think, "Who made it?" And you can say *(pause for response)*, "God did!" When you see a spider *(show them the spider)*, say, "Who made it?" *(Pause for response.)* "God did!" When you see some leaves *(show them the leaves)*, say, "Who made them?" *(Pause for response.)* "God did!" And these flowers—"who made them?" *(Pause for response.)* "God did!"

Anywhere you go outside, anything you see, you can point to it, think about who made it, and say *(pause for response)*, "God did." And if anyone asks you who made the world and everything in it, what will you say? *(Pause for response.)* Yes! "GOD DID!"

The Sun Forever

Scripture: Never will I leave you; never will I forsake you (Heb. 13:5).

Concept: God is always with us.

Object: None. (*Note:* It's good to know ahead of time where in the sanctuary sunlight hits the floor. Have the children sit in that spot. Provisions are made for both sunny and cloudy days and for buildings into which the sun doesn't shine. On a cloudy day, use option 1.)

Song: "No, Never Alone."

Option 1

I wanted us to sit in sunlight today but the sun isn't out. This is where the sun would shine if it were out.

Option 2

(*In a building without windows say,*) I wanted us to sit in the sunlight today, but the sun doesn't shine into this building. Look around the sanctuary (*or* room) for a minute. (*Pause while the children look around.*) Do you see any sunlight? (*Pause for response.*)

Just because you don't see sunlight, does that mean that the sun isn't shining today? *(Pause for response.)* Of course not! We just can't see the sun inside this building.

Now, pretend that we're sitting outside but the sun isn't out.

Option 3

(On a sunny day, say,) I thought it would be nice to sit in the sunlight this morning, it feels so warm and cozy here. Besides that, I'd like to talk about the sun for a little while.

It's a bright, sunny day today; the sun is out. But what about days when the sun isn't out? Pretend that we're sitting here and there isn't any sunlight. Pretend the sun isn't out today.

Continue Lesson

When the sun isn't out, has it disappeared from the sky? Is it gone completely? *(Pause for response.)* Of course not! It's still there. Some days, clouds get in the way and we can't see the sun. Is there ever a day when the sun isn't in the sky? *(Pause for response.)* No! The sun is always up there.

How about at night? When the sun sets and it gets dark outside, has the sun dropped out of the sky? *(Pause for response.)* No! It disappears from our side of the world, but it's shining on the other side of the world. The sun is still in the sky; we just can't see it.

Does the sun ever, ever drop out of the sky? *(Pause for response.)* No! That's a silly question, isn't it? The sun is always up in the sky. We can't see it all the time, but it's there.

Let's talk for a minute about what the sun does. Does it help plants grow? *(Pause for response.)* Yes! Green plants can't grow without the sun. If the sun didn't shine, we wouldn't have food. Does the sun give us heat? *(Pause for response.)* Yes! You probably feel warm right now, don't you? Without the sun, everything outside would be frozen. Does the sun give us light? *(Pause for response.)* Yes! Without the sun, every day would be darker than most of our nights. Do you think we need the sun to be able to live? *(Pause for response.)* Yes! We wouldn't be able to live on earth if the sun weren't here.

But we don't have to worry about that. The sun won't disappear, it will always be up in the sky.

Sometimes I think maybe God put the sun in the sky to remind us of him, because God is always here too. God won't disappear. In a way, God is like the sun, only much, much better.

God has promised us that he will never leave us. Sometimes it may seem like God isn't nearby. That's like a cloudy day, or like night, when we can't see the sun. Do you think God is really gone? *(Pause for response.)* No! Maybe we're not thinking about God or praying to him. That's like clouds in the sky or a sunset. But God is still here, even when we don't think about him. He's promised to be with us always.

Just like we need the sun for life, we need God. Who made us and gives us life? Who gave us the sun? *(Pause for response.)* Of course, God! Who loves us and promises to take care of us? *(Pause for response.)* God does! So, who do we need for our lives? *(Pause for response.)* Yes, God!

I know that God didn't put the sun in the sky just to remind us of him, but it is a good reminder. Whenever we see the sun or look for it, we can think of God, who gives us life and who promised never, never to leave us.

Body and Soul

Scripture: If there is a natural body, there is also a spiritual body (1 Cor. 15:44).

Concept: Our physical bodies are "shells" that cover our real selves inside.

Objects: Shells (snail, clam, turtle, any seashells). (*Note:* Provision is made for using one snail shell or several shells.)

Who can tell me what this is? (*Hold up a shell. Pause for response.*) Yes, it's a snail shell. I picked it up at the pond (*or wherever*) this week and took it along to show you.

The shell is empty now, there's nothing living inside it. Yet, I know that it's a snail shell. I can tell by looking at it that a snail once lived in here.

Option 1

(If you have only one shell, you may want to include two or three extra facts about that one shell at this point. You can talk about the shell itself, the colors, the shape, where the creature peered in and out; how the creature added to the shell as it grew; how the shell protected the creature, etc.)

Option 2

(If you have several shells, you may want to show the individual shells. With each shell stress that it's empty, but you know what kind of creature lived in it by looking at the shell. Then select one shell with which to continue.)

Continue Lesson

(Hold up a shell.) Is this a snail? *(Pause for response.)* No, it isn't. It's only the shell. It was part of the snail when the snail was alive. But the real snail, the part that ate and moved and thought snail thoughts, was inside the shell. There's much more to a snail than just this shell.

If the snail were still in the shell, I could hold it up and say, "This is a snail." But now the snail part of the snail is gone. This is just the shell. The snail just lived in the shell.

That's sort of like people, isn't it? There's much more to people than just the "shells," or bodies, that you see. You can't see how a person thinks, or feels, or loves, can you? That's all on the inside person.

The Bible tells us that we have our bodies that we can see, and we have our souls, the inside person, that we can't see. The real you is inside of your body. The real you is the part that thinks, and learns, and feels, and loves. Your body is just a covering for the real you.

(Hold up the shell or shells.) Some of you may think this shell is pretty, and some of you may not like it at all. (*Or,* Some of these shells are pretty and some, I

think, are not so pretty.) But that didn't matter at all to the snail (creatures) inside, did it?

That's just like people, too, isn't it? Does it matter if you're tall or short, if you have curly hair or straight, if your shell is brown or white? *(Pause for response.)* Of course not! The real you is inside that shell. The real you is what matters.

People recognize you by your shell, by the way you look. They look at you and say, "There's Ryan," or "There's Emily." But what really matters is what Ryan or Emily is like inside. Are they loving people? Are they helpful, cheerful people?

We all look different; we all have different shells. But that doesn't matter, because the real us is on the inside. I think that's really special. It's not important to be tall or to be pretty; that's only our bodies. It's important to have love inside, to love Jesus; because that comes from the real us inside, from our souls.

The next time you see some shells, or even a creature in a shell, that can remind you of yourself. The shells are coverings; the real creature is inside. You, too, are body and soul. Your body's just a shell. It's what's inside you that counts.

30

Who Counts the Stars?

Scripture: He determines the number of the stars and calls them each by name. Great is our Lord and mighty in power; his understanding has no limit (Ps. 147:4–5).

Concept: God can do anything and knows everything.

Objects: Many little silver stars pasted on a piece of black paper. It's nice, but not necessary, to have a star on a piece of paper for each child. (*Note:* This lesson deals with three aspects of stars—numbers, size, and distance—and is too advanced for very young children. You may want to deal with only one aspect.)

Song: "Twinkle, Twinkle Little Star," "Little Stars Are Shining."

What have I pasted on this paper? (*Hold up the paper so the children can see it. Pause for response.*) Stars, lots of stars! There are probably more stars here than we want to count right now.

Let's count a few. (*Point to a few as you count them, slowly, for the children to count with you.*) One, two, three, four . . . that's enough. You get the idea. There are too many stars here to count right now.

I brought these stars to remind us of the real stars we see at night. Have you ever gone outside at night and tried to count all the stars you see? It's impossible, isn't it? There are just too many stars.

If you tried to count all the stars in the sky like this, one, two, three, four . . . *(count at about one per second; point to the stars on the paper as you count),* you would have to count for your whole life, and you still wouldn't count all the stars. You could probably count these paper stars in one night. But you couldn't count real stars in your lifetime. There are billions and billions of stars. No one knows how many there are.

Wait! One person knows. Who knows how many stars there are in the sky? *(Pause for response.)* That's right, God knows. The Bible says that God knows the number of stars and counts them all by name. There are more stars than we can count, yet God knows them all.

(Hold up the paper again.) These stars are small enough to hold in your hand, but real stars aren't. They're much bigger than that. Can anyone guess how big real stars are? Are they bigger than this church? *(Pause for response. Encourage some guesses with a few questions.)* Are they bigger than a mountain? Are they bigger than this city? Are they bigger than our world?

Real stars are much bigger than our whole wide world. They're bigger than we can imagine. They're also hotter than we can imagine, hotter than our sun. And they're brighter than we can imagine. If stars were close to you, you'd go blind, they're so bright. They're brighter than our sun. We really can't even imagine how big or hot or bright stars are.

Who can imagine that? Who made the stars and knows all about them? *(Pause for response.)* Of course; the Bible tells us that God made the stars. God knows all about things that are too big for us to imagine.

(Hold up the paper again.) These stars are close enough to touch, but real stars aren't. They're far, far, away. If you got into a car and tried to ride to the nearest star *(lead their imaginations upward with your hand),* how long do you think it would take? *(Pause for response. Encourage some guesses with a few questions.)* Would it take a day? A week? A year, of riding all the time?

Stars are so far away that we could never reach them by car. That would take millions of years. We probably can never reach the stars any way we travel, they're so far away. They're farther away than we can imagine.

Yet, who knows exactly how far away the stars are? *(Pause for response.)* Yes, God does! God made the stars and counts the stars and knows exactly how far away they are. We can't even imagine that, but God knows it.

Is there anything that God doesn't know? *(Pause for response.)* No! God knows everything. Knowing all about the stars is just one little part of what God knows. God knows absolutely everything.

God can do all things. God can make stars bigger and brighter than we can imagine. He can count the stars with numbers way too big for us. But that's just a little bit of what God can do. There's nothing that's too big or too hard for God to do. God can do anything.

So, if you go outside tonight and look at the stars, they can remind you of God. Who made the stars and can also make or do anything else? *(Pause for response.)* God! Who knows all about the stars and knows everything else there is to know? *(Pause for response.)* God! Look at the stars, and know how great God is.

Option

(Add the following paragraph if you have stars for the children.)

I have a star (a few stars) for each of you to take home with you today. Put them someplace where you will see them during the day, when you can't see real stars. Then you can be reminded both day and night of how great God is.

31

Protected by Feathers

Scripture: He will cover you with his feathers, and under his wings you will find refuge (Ps. 91:4).

Concept: God protects us as parent birds protect their young.

Objects: A feather (a large quill-like feather would be best, but any will do), a glass of water (optional).

Can you all see this? *(Hold up the feather.)* What is it? *(Pause for response.)* Yes, it's a feather. Some bird was changing its feathers; it dropped this one and grew a new one instead. This feather doesn't do much all by itself. But combined with other feathers, it's super protection for a bird.

Feathers are waterproof; they shed rain. *(If you have some water handy, put just a drop on top of the feather to show how water won't soak through.)* When a bird is caught in the rain, does its body become wet? *(Pause for response.)* No, its feathers keep it dry.

Feathers also keep a bird warm. They trap heat right next to the bird's body. In fact, we use down feathers in some of our winter jackets and bed quilts because they keep us so warm.

Parent birds protect their babies with feathers, don't they? A parent bird will sit on a nest, spread its wings *(make appropriate motions)*, and where will the baby birds hide? *(Pause for response.)* Yes, under the parent's wings. There they'll stay safe and warm and dry. They're safe because they're with their parent; they're warm and dry because they're under their parent's wingfeathers.

The Bible says that God will protect us the same way. It says that God will cover us with his feathers, and we'll be protected under his wings.

Does God really have feathers and wings? *(Pause for response.)* I don't think so. The Bible is using picture language here. Picture words help us understand God. *(Show the feather.)* We know that feathers keep birds warm and dry. And we know that parent birds spread their wings to protect their young. So the Bible uses those picture words to tell us that God will take good care of us. A parent bird protects its young as well as it can; so God will take care of us, too.

(Show them the feather again.) So this feather, or any feather you see, is a picture promise to you. When you see a feather, think of a parent bird protecting its young; then remember that God will protect you.

God's Stop Signs

Scripture: You shall not murder. You shall not commit adultery. You shall not steal. You shall not give false testimony. . . . You shall not covet . . . (Exod. 20:13–17).

Concept: God tells us not to do certain things, for our own good.

Object: A picture of a stop sign. (*Note:* A rough drawing is fine, as long as it's the proper shape and an obvious red.)

Song: "Oh Be Careful."

Who can tell me what this is? *(Hold up the picture. Pause for response.)* Of course, it's a stop sign. You can tell by the shape and color that it's a stop sign. You can't miss a stop sign; it's always red and it's always this shape. People make stop signs that shape and color so that you can recognize it.

What must you do when you see a stop sign? *(Pause for response.)* That's right, you must stop. When Mom or Dad drives a car down the street, they stop at this sign. Then they look very carefully before they go on. Even when you're walking, you should stop at this sign. If you don't, you may be in trouble.

What might happen if someone ignores a stop sign? What if they just went walking right past it into traffic? *(Pause for response.)* Yes, they might have an accident.

That stop sign is there for a reason. It usually means that there's traffic ahead and you should be very careful. If you ignore the stop sign you might have an accident. You may be hurt. That stop sign is there for your own good, isn't it? It's there to warn you that you should be very careful.

Did you know that God put some stop signs in the Bible, too? He did! Just like these stop signs *(hold up the picture)*, God's stop signs are there to warn us. They're in the Bible for our own good.

Just like these stop signs *(hold up the picture)*, God's stop signs are easy to recognize. God's stop signs usually say, "You shall not . . ." Whenever you hear a "You shall not" from the Bible, you're at one of God's stop signs.

Can anyone think of a "You shall not"? *(Pause for response.)* How about "You shall not steal" or "You shall not lie"? Do you think those are God's stop signs? *(Nod your head and pause for response.)* Yes, they are. Those stop signs are very easy to recognize, aren't they? They say, "You shall not . . ." They tell you about things you shouldn't do.

Why did God put some stop signs in the Bible? Is it just because he wants to give us a lot of rules? *(Shake your head and pause for response.)* Of course not! God put stop signs in the Bible because he loves us.

Do you think you would get into a lot of trouble if you stole or lied? *(Pause for response.)* Of course. We're not going to talk about all that trouble today; but we know that stealing and telling lies are not good things.

God doesn't want to see us get into trouble. God loves us, so to keep us out of trouble, he tells us not to do certain things. He wants us to be good people, so he put those stop signs in the Bible to help us. God loves us so much he wants only good for us, so he helps us stay away from bad things.

I'd like you to try something on your way home from church today. Count all the stop signs. *(Hold up the picture.)* You'll recognize them by their shape and color.

Then, with each stop sign, think about one of God's stop signs. You'll know them by the words, "You shall not . . ."

As you stop at each stop sign on the streets, remember that they're there for your own good. That can remind you of God's stop signs. They're in the Bible because God loves you and wants the best for you.

33

Well-Planted?

Scripture: This is what the LORD says: Cursed is the one who trusts in man, who depends on flesh for his strength. . . . He will be like a bush in the wastelands; . . . But blessed is the man who trusts in the LORD, whose confidence is in him. He will be like a tree planted by the water that sends out its roots by the stream (Jer. 17:5–8).

Concept: You live best when you trust in the Lord.

Objects: Two houseplants of the same kind. Repot one into sandbox sand. Give it very little water. Be sure the other is in good soil and well-tended. (*Note:* This should be done a few weeks before this lesson so that the difference in the plants is obvious.)

I've got two plants here that are the same kind. *(Show them the plants.)* They're both (<u>name of the plant</u>). They don't look at all alike, do they? This one *(indicate the plant in sand)* looks terrible. It isn't growing well at all. But this one *(indicate the plant in soil)* is doing just fine.

116

What, do you think, is the difference? *(As you ask the question, tilt the pots slightly so that they can see the soil and the sand. Pause for response. How you proceed depends on the response.)* I didn't water this one well? That's true, I didn't water it well. I tended the healthy plant a little more carefully. I think there's more. Look closely at what's in the pots. Not enough sunlight on the sick one? Probably. I didn't make sure that it got enough sun. But there's more. Look at the soil around each plant.

What's in this pot? *(Indicate the sick plant and let them see the sand.)* That's right, sand! Most plants don't grow well in sand. There's not enough food in sand for plants to live well.

What's in this pot? *(Indicate the healthy plant and let them see the good soil.)* Yes, good, rich soil! This has lots of minerals for the plant to use. It holds water well, and I watered it enough so that the plant could drink. It also anchors the plant well. It's just good, healthy soil for the plant to grow.

Where a plant grows, *where* it puts down roots, makes a big difference in *how* it grows. If it grows in a really sandy place without much water, like this *(indicate the plant in sand)*, it probably won't do too well. But if it puts down roots in good soil by lots of water, like this *(indicate the plant in soil)*, it should be healthy.

Did you know that God once compared us to plants like these? He did! God said that where *we* put down roots, where we put our trust, makes a big difference in how we grow as Christians.

God said that someone who trusts only in other people, who looks only to people to tell them what is right and wrong, grows like this plant. *(Indicate the plant in the sand.)* It's growing in no-good soil, like a plant in a desert. People don't always give you good advice. People don't always stand by you. Some people love themselves more than you. So you don't grow right as a Christian when you only trust in people. You're like a plant *(indicate the scrawny plant once more)* growing in a wasteland.

(Put the scrawny plant firmly behind you and pick up the good plant.) Someone who trusts in the Lord grows like this plant. God said that they're like a tree planted by water. You can trust the Lord always to guide you, through the Bible. God tells you in the Bible that he will never fail you. And he promises always to love you. You're like a healthy plant growing by a stream in good soil if you trust in God.

The next time you see a scrawny plant *(indicate your scrawny plant)* trying to grow with hardly anything around it, check it out. The soil probably is poor. It's not well-planted. And when you see a lush garden with lots of healthy plants *(indicate the healthy plant)*, check out that soil. It's probably nice and rich and well-watered.

Then you can think about where you are planted. Do you trust the Lord? Then you are well-planted *(indicate the healthy plant)*, becoming a healthy Christian.

Family Pictures

Scripture: The Spirit himself testifies with our spirit that we are God's children (Rom. 8:16).

Concept: Christians are siblings; God is our parent.

Objects: Pictures of a few (three or four) families. (*Note:* These can be real photos or pictures from magazines. Try to include at least one single-parent family. Do not include any families of children who might be present.)

Song: "I'm So Glad I'm a Part of the Family of God."

I brought a few pictures of families with me today, because I thought it would be nice to talk about our families.

(*Show a picture.*) Here are Mom and Dad. This is _____, and that's his sister, _____. This is the _____ family. Their last name comes from (<u>the mom's or dad's or both</u>) last name. All the children belong to Mom and Dad, so they have the same last name.

(*Go through all the family pictures using the same basic formula: Point out the parent(s); name the siblings, pointing out that they are brothers and sisters;*

119

give their last name, based on the parent's last name. With the single-parent family, point out that many families have only one parent; some may have none. But children are never left alone; there is always someone in charge. If siblings have different last names, point out that they were named after who was their parent when they were born. Someone else may be a parent and in charge now.)

These pictures are of families that you don't know very well. Let's talk about your families for a minute.

Raise your hand if you have any brothers. *(Demonstrate and pause for response.)* Some of you have brothers, and some don't. Now raise your hand if you have any sisters. *(Demonstrate and pause for response.)* Some have sisters and some don't. Now raise your hand if you know your last name. *(Demonstrate and pause for response.)* That's always one of the first things you learn, isn't it? Your parents always teach you your last name.

Does anyone here know if he or she has a family picture at home? Do you have a photograph of your whole family? Raise your hand if you do. *(Pause for response.)* Some do, some don't. Maybe you're not sure if you have a family picture or not.

I want to show you a kind of picture of your whole family. This is going to be a surprise, because it's not just your mom and dad. This is your whole family that Jesus gave you. It's so big, I couldn't fit it on a picture. But you can see that big family in a living picture. Just look out there. *(Point to the congregation. Include the entire group with a sweep of your arm.)*

All those people out there are sisters and brothers that Jesus gave you. They're all part of your family, and you're part of their family. You can call any person out there "brother" or "sister," and you would be right.

Do some of them seem rather old to be your brothers and sisters? Probably; but some people have rather old sisters and brothers. You do; just look out there.

Do you want to say that they're not really related to you? You know them, and they're nice people, but they're not your brothers and sisters? Well, the Bible says that we are God's children. If God is our parent and we are all his children, aren't we sisters and brothers? (*Nod and pause for response.*) Of course we are! God made us one big family.

Who's in charge of our family? (*Pause for response.*) That's right, God is. God loves us, his children, very much. And God wants us to love each other, our brothers and sisters in Christ.

What is our last name? I just gave you a little hint. We are all brothers and sisters in Christ, and our name is . . . (*pause for response*) yes, Christian. If you are a Christian, you are a part of this great big family. (*Indicate the whole congregation.*)

So, brothers and sisters (*look directly at the children*), will you do this (brother *or* sister) two little favors today? I'd be very happy if you did.

First, after you go back to your seat, listen very carefully to how we pray, how we talk to God. I think you'll hear the pastor call God our Father. And that's just what he is. God is our loving Father.

Second, after the service is over today, find a boy or girl who sat near you. Go up to that person and respectfully say, "Hello, brother" or "Hello, sister," because that's what they are. They're part of your family. We're all sisters and brothers in Christ.

The Real Stuff's Inside

Scripture: Man looks at the outward appearance, but the LORD looks at the heart (1 Sam. 16:7).

Concept: God considers our hearts as the real us.

Objects: A few acorns and a few peanuts. Any two kinds of nuts (or even their shells) will do. In a pinch you can do this with one kind of nut and let the children imagine the peanuts.

I picked up these nuts last week. *(Show the acorns.)* What kind of nuts are they? *(Pause for response.)* That's right, they're acorns. If I planted these acorns, what kind of trees would grow? *(Pause for response.)* Yes, oak trees. Acorns come from oak trees; they're really seeds for new oak trees.

(Show the peanuts.) If I buried a peanut, what kind of plant would grow? *(Pause for response.)* A peanut plant. Whatever kind of nut you bury, that's the kind of plant that grows. Oak trees come from acorns; peanut plants come from peanuts.

(Show the acorns again.) If I planted just the acorn cap, would I get an oak tree? *(Pause for response.)* How

about an acorn shell, an acorn with nothing inside? Would that give me a tree? *(Pause for response.)* Of course not! You need the inside of the nut to get a tree.

(Show the peanuts.) Would I get a peanut plant if I buried a few empty peanut shells? *(Pause for response.)* No! The peanut itself sprouts into a plant. Just the shell does no good. The real stuff's inside. You need the inside stuff to grow a new plant.

(Show the acorns again.) Squirrels love acorns, don't they? Do they eat the shells or the insides? *(Pause for response.)* They eat the insides! Squirrels can pull acorns apart to get at the good stuff, the real nut, inside.

(Show the peanuts.) When you eat peanuts, do you eat the shells or the insides? *(Pause for response.)* Of course, you eat the insides. Usually you throw the shells away.

You get the idea, don't you? It's the nut itself, inside the shell, that counts. The real stuff that grows into plants or that provides food is inside. The shell is only a shell.

In a way, we're just like these nuts. It's what's inside us that counts. God tells us that he looks at our hearts. God knows that the real us is inside, and that's what he cares about.

Do you think it matters to God if you're shaped like this acorn, or wrinkled like this peanut shell? *(Indicate the nuts and pause for response.)* Of course not! You're not shaped like a nut and you don't look like a nut, but it wouldn't matter if you did. Your body is only your shell. God looks right past that to the inside.

Does it matter to God if you're healthy inside? Does he care if you love him and if you love others? *(Pause for response.)* Of course! God tells us that he looks at our hearts. He looks at the real us, inside. That's what he cares about.

So, the next time you find an acorn or pick up a peanut, look at it for just a minute and think of yourself. That outer shell doesn't mean much. Try to crack it open and look at the inside to see if you have a good nut. *(Crack a peanut.)* And while you're doing that you can remember that God looks through your shell at your heart, the real you. *(Show the nutmeat.)* The real stuff is inside.

36

Jesus Is the Key

Scripture: Whoever believes in him is not condemned, but whoever does not believe stands condemned already because he has not believed in the name of God's one and only Son (John 3:18).

Concept: Jesus is the only way to heaven.

Objects: Keys (car, house, shed or bathroom door, and workplace keys work well).

Can you see what I have here? *(Show your car key. Pause for response.)* Yes, it's a key. It's my car key. What do I use this key for? *(Pause for response.)* I use it to get into my car, that's right! And I use it to start my car.

(Show the house key.) This is my house key. Can I get into my car or start it with this key? *(Pause for response.)* Of course not! This is the key to my house, not my car. It doesn't fit my car.

(Show the car key again.) I lost this car key for a little while yesterday, and I was really worried. Do you know why? *(Pause for response.)* Of course! The car was locked and I couldn't get in without the key. I can't use another key *(show the house key)*, I need

this one *(show the car key)*. I can't get into my car without the key.

(Show the house key.) This is the key to my house. It's the only key I have and my house is locked up tightly. It's very secure. Can I get into my house without this key? *(Shake your head to encourage the right response.)* No! What must I use to get into my house? *(Hold up the key as you ask.)* Yes, the key! It's the only way to get in.

Option

(If you have older children in your audience, you may want to use the following paragraph. If the children are young, you may want to skip this rather than introduce another element.)

Of course, I could break into my house, couldn't I? But I've made it quite secure. Almost no one can get in without the key or else breaking down part of the house.

Continue Lesson

(Show the shed key.) This is the key to the shed in my backyard. It's the only key I have, and my shed is locked up tightly. It's very secure. Can I get into my shed without this key? *(Shake your head to encourage the right response.)* No! What must I use to get into my shed? *(Hold up the key as you ask.)* Yes, the key! It's the only way to get in.

(Show the workplace key.) This is the key to my office. It's the only key I have, and my office is locked up tightly. It's very secure. Can I get into my office without this key? *(Shake your head to encourage the right response.)*

No! What must I use to get into my office? *(Hold up the key as you ask.)* Yes, the key! It's the only way to get in.

Keys are very important, aren't they? You can't get into some places without a key, and only one certain key will let you in.

That's like heaven; one key will let you in. Who is our key to heaven? *(Pause for response. You may have to prompt them with the following questions.)* Who came to earth to save us? Who died for our sins? "Believe on the Lord" who? "and you shall be saved."

Yes, Jesus! Jesus is our key to heaven. He paid for our sins so that we can live with him in heaven. The Bible says that Jesus is the only way to heaven. Jesus is our key.

Can we get into heaven without the key, without Jesus? *(Shake your head to encourage the right response.)* No! Heaven is very secure. There's no other way to get in. Jesus is the key.

If we believe in Jesus and love him, we will someday live with him in heaven. If we don't believe in him and don't love him, we've lost the key.

(Hold up all the keys at once.) We have all sorts of keys, don't we? We need them to get into certain places. Each key lets us into one place, so we need a whole bunch of keys.

But who is the only key to heaven? *(Pause for response.)* Yes, Jesus. He's the only key. If you love Jesus, you have the key.

Practice Pennies

Scripture: God loves a cheerful giver
(2 Cor. 9:7).

Concept: God wants us to give cheerfully.

Objects: Pennies, enough for each child to have
one; an offering plate.

I brought some pennies with me today. Each of you may have one for just a little while. *(Continue to speak as you pass out the pennies.)* Put the pennies down quietly in front of you for a few minutes. They're only practice pennies. We're going to practice something with them in just a little while.

First, we're going to practice something else. We're going to practice being cheerful. The Bible often tells us to be cheerful. It usually doesn't say "Be cheerful"; it says, "Be of good cheer." Jesus often said, "Be of good cheer." That meant, "Be cheerful."

Look at my face. *(Frown at them.)* Does this look cheerful? *(Pause for response.)* No! It looks grumpy, doesn't it?

Look at this. *(Smile brightly.)* Does this look cheerful? *(Pause for response.)* It sure does. This looks a lot better. If you're really cheerful, you usually look like this. *(Smile brightly again.)*

Since the Bible tells us to be cheerful, let's practice looking cheerful. Let's see you all smile nice, big smiles. *(Pause for response.)* That's wonderful!

Now, just to feel the difference, try a frown. *(Frown at them and pause for response.)* That doesn't look so good, does it?

Let's look cheerful instead. Can you put on a cheerful smile? *(Pause for response.)* That's great. At least you look cheerful. That's a beginning to being cheerful. And God wants us to be cheerful.

Besides talking about being cheerful, God says a lot about giving. God tells us to give to the poor. We should share what we have. God has promised that if we give what we have, God will give us more yet. God tells us all sorts of things about how we should give.

One thing God tells us is that he loves a cheerful giver. You already practiced looking cheerful, didn't you? Let's see those cheerful smiles again. *(Pause for response.)* That looks great.

Now we'll practice cheerful giving. Remember that I said those pennies were practice pennies? We're going to give those to God when we practice being cheerful givers.

(Show them the offering plate.) You've all seen this, haven't you? This is an offering plate, where we put money that we give to God (*or* the church, *or you may want to name a few offerings*). So, to practice cheerful giving we'll be cheerful (*smile brightly at them as you put a penny in the plate*) as we give.

I'll pass the plate around. You put your penny in it while you smile a big smile. *(Continue to speak as you pass the plate to the children.)* Thank you! Those are wonderful smiles. You look like really cheerful givers. God loves cheerful givers.

I keep saying you *look* like cheerful givers. I can't make you cheerful by telling you to smile, but it's a good step in the right direction. You can smile when you share your toys with a friend, or when you give someone a toy. Smile brightly; be a cheerful giver.

The next time you see this offering plate come down your row (*or* you see people putting offerings in this plate), look at faces. Are people cheerful? Then, as you put in your offering, smile brightly; God loves you. God loves a cheerful giver.

Who's the Greatest?

Scripture: Now you are the body of Christ, and each one of you is a part of it (1 Cor. 12:27).

Concept: All members of Christ's church are equally important.

Object: None; use the children themselves.

I'd like you to try a few experiments with me. We want to find out a little bit more about our bodies.

Now that you're sitting down, try this. Very quietly, stand up and try to stand on only one leg. Do it very quietly, like this. *(Demonstrate and pause while they try.)* OK, you may sit down. That was rather difficult, wasn't it? It's easier to stand on two legs than on only one.

Pretend for a minute that I asked you to hop back to your seat on only one leg. That would probably be more difficult than standing on one leg, wouldn't it? What would happen if you had no legs? You wouldn't be able to stand up at all. You surely wouldn't be able to walk back to your seats, would you? Do you think that your legs are an important part of your body? *(Nod and pause for response.)* Of course they are. You can't stand or walk without your legs.

Is one leg more important than the other leg, or are both legs important? *(Pause for response.)* Yes, both legs are important. One is no more important than the other. You need both legs to stand and to walk.

Now, close your eyes for a minute. Are they closed? Keep them closed while you try to look around the church and find your seat. *(Pause for just a minute.)* That's silly, isn't it? You can't see with your eyes closed. OK, you may open them. Pretend for a minute that I asked you to walk back to your seat with your eyes closed. Could you find your seat without using your eyes? *(Pause for response.)* Probably not. Someone would have to lead you to your seat. Do you think that your eyes are an important part of your body? *(Nod and pause for response.)* Of course they are. You can't see where you're going without your eyes.

What's more important, your eyes or your two legs? *(Pause briefly.)* That's impossible to answer, isn't it? Your eyes and your legs are both important. One is not more important than the other.

We're going to pretend a little bit more. Pretend that I'm giving each of you a juicy red apple. *(Pretend to put one in front of each child as you speak.)* I'm setting one apple in front of each of you. Don't pick it up yet; just look at it. OK. Pretend that you want to eat that apple, but you have no hands. Try to pick it up without using your hands. *(Demonstrate and pause while they try.)* That's difficult, isn't it? Your hands are really important.

Now you have hands, but you have no elbows. You may pick up that apple and try to eat it. Don't bend your elbows; pretend that you have none.

133

(Demonstrate and pause while they try.) Well, I guess elbows are important, too. You can't eat that apple without bending your elbows.

What's more important, your hands or your elbows? *(Pause briefly.)* That's impossible to answer, isn't it? Both are important. You need both to eat that pretend apple.

Every part of your body is important. Each part is different, but each part is important. And they work together to help you walk back to your seat or eat that pretend apple. All those important parts work together for your body.

That's just like this church, these people. *(Indicate the complete congregation, including the children, as you speak.)* Every person here is an important part of the church. We call this the (name of your church), not the (name of your minister or some families) church, don't we? No one is more important than anyone else here.

The Bible tells us that we, the church, are the body of Christ. Each one of us is an important part. No one is more important than anyone else.

(Your minister) is important, right? *(Nod and pause for response.)* We need someone to tell us about God's Word. But could we sit and listen if the doors were locked or if it were cold in here? *(Pause for response.)* Of course not! So (your custodian) is very important, too. Would you stay here for Sunday school if there were no teachers? *(Pause for response.)* No! So (names of Sunday school teachers) are important, too. But could they be Sunday school teachers if there were no kids for Sunday school?

(Pause for response.) Of course not! So you and you and you *(point to various children)* are important, too.

Each one of us is important in Christ's church. You are just as important here as anyone else. No one is more important than anyone else. Each one of us has special things that we can do in the church. And all together we make up the church, the body of Christ.

That's just like your body, isn't it? Every body part is important. No part is more important than any other. All parts work together.

Option

(If the children are older, say,) I'd like you to try one more little experiment. You may stand up quietly. *(If they are on stairs, direct them to the bottom.)* Close your eyes and take four steps toward your seats. *(Pause while they try.)* OK, open your eyes. Take four steps toward your seats without bending your knees. *(Pause while they do so.)* You may stop. Now, take three hops toward your seat on one leg. *(Pause while they do so.)* I think you get the idea.

Continue Lesson

You, like everyone else, are an important member of this church. Now you may walk normally back to your seats.

Ever Green, Ever Living

Scripture: For God so loved the world that he gave his one and only Son, that whoever believes in him shall not perish but have eternal life (John 3:16).

Concept: If we believe in Jesus we shall live forever.

Object: A twig, with needles still attached, from an evergreen tree. (*Note:* You can substitute a picture of an evergreen tree for the twig. Skip the first sentence only.)

Song: "For God So Loved the World."

I took this twig from a tree I passed this week. Can anyone tell me what kind of tree it is? *(Show the twig and pause for response.)* That's right, it's a pine (*or a spruce, or whatever*). If we don't know exactly the kind of tree, we call any tree with needles an evergreen.

Why do we call this an evergreen? *(Pause for response.)* Yes, because the tree is always green. Some trees drop their leaves and look like they're dead during the winter. But this tree doesn't drop its needles; it's always green. It looks like it never dies, because it's always green. That's why we call it an evergreen: ever green *(hold up the twig)*, ever living.

In a way, you can be just like an evergreen tree. You can always, always be alive. Your body will die someday, but the real you inside your body will live forever and ever. The real you will never die. God has promised you that.

How can the real you live forever? *(Pause for response. You may have to lead them with the next questions.)* Who did God send to save us from our sins? Who do we believe in to live forever? Jesus! The Bible says that whoever believes in Jesus shall have eternal life. That means that if you believe that Jesus died for your sins, the real you won't ever die. You can always live, with him.

(Show them the twig again.) So this can be a good reminder. What is this called? *(Pause for response.)* Yes, an evergreen. Ever green, ever living. It's just like the real you, ever living because of Jesus.

This week, if you see one of these trees—an evergreen—say to yourself, "Ever green, ever living." Then thank Jesus that your soul, the real you, will live forever because of him.

No Branch Alone

Scripture: I am the vine; you are the branches
. . . apart from me you can do nothing (John
15:5).

Concept: Christians absolutely need Jesus.

Object: A tree branch or large twig.

I picked up this branch from my yard (*or* churchyard *or* field) a few days ago. *(Hold up the branch for all to see. Keep it within view while talking about it.)* It must have come from a nearby tree. Maybe the wind blew it down, or someone cracked it off, or it just fell off because it was dead. I don't know, but here's the branch.

The leaves are starting to wither already. (*Or* The leaves are dead; *or* There are no leaves on it.) If I keep this branch for a while, will it grow new green leaves? *(Pause for response.)* No, it won't! This branch will never grow another leaf.

This branch probably once grew some nuts or some fruit or maybe some seeds. Can it do that again? If I keep this branch for a while, will it grow new fruit? *(Pause for response.)* No, it won't! This branch will never grow another seed.

Why can't this branch make any new leaves or seeds? *(Pause for response.)* That's right, because it's dead. A dead branch can't do anything.

Why is it dead? *(Pause for response. You may have to lead the children with a few questions.)* Can this branch live all by itself? No, it has to be connected to something. What must the branch be connected to? Yes, a branch must be connected to a tree in order to live.

A branch can't live by itself. To stay alive, a branch absolutely needs a tree. It must be connected to the tree. That's the only way it can get food and water and everything it needs to live. A branch alone is a dead branch; a branch connected to a tree can live.

(Put the branch down.) Jesus called us branches; did you know that? He said, "I am the vine, you are the branches." He could have said, "I am a tree, you are the branches." He went on to say, "Apart from me you can do nothing."

If we are the branches, who is the tree? *(Pause for response.)* That's right. Jesus is the tree. Just as this branch *(hold up the branch)* needs a tree, so we need Jesus.

There are no Christians without Jesus. Jesus saved us from our sins. Without him, we're as dead to God as this branch. Christians absolutely need Jesus. We must stay connected to him.

Option

(If the children are very young, skip the next paragraph to avoid introducing a second concept.)

How do we stay connected to Jesus? *(Pause for response. You may have to prompt them with a few ques-*

tions.) Do we pray to him? Do we read Bible stories about him? Do we think about him? Sure, we do all of those. We believe that Jesus saves us from sin, and we talk to him every day. That's how we stay connected to Jesus.

Continue Lesson

(Hold up the branch.) I guess I'll throw this branch away. It's no good anymore; it's not connected to the tree. If you see any branches on the ground this week, you might as well pick them up and throw them away too. But, when you do, remember that you also are a branch. Who is the tree? *(Pause for response.)* That's right, Jesus is the tree.

All you branches can go back to your seats now. And when you get there, maybe you can say a little prayer to Jesus, the tree, to stay connected to him.

Solid as a Rock

Scripture: You are my Father, my God, the Rock my Savior (Ps. 89:26).

Concept: God is as solid and changeless as a rock.

Object: A large rock.

Song: "Rock of Ages," "The Lord's My Rock."

I took this rock from a nearby field yesterday. *(Hold up the rock so the children can see it.)* I'm sure it's been there for years, but I picked it up to show to you. Let's talk about rocks for a minute.

Do you think this rock has changed at all since I picked it up? *(Pause for response.)* No! It looks exactly the same as it did the first time I saw it. Rocks don't change, do they? I can beat on it *(pound the rock with your fists)*, and it won't change. Rain can pour on it, and it won't change. Wind can blow over it *(blow hard on the rock)*, and it won't change. It's solid; it won't change.

Pretend for a minute that this rock is much bigger than you are. *(Indicate a huge boulder with your hands. Mimic actions of the next sentences.)* You can stand up straight behind it and it will hide you completely. You can climb to the top, but it's way above your head. It's so big you can squeeze under part of it. It's a huge, solid rock.

Now pretend that there's a sudden storm. *(Make rain motions with your hands.)* Where can you go to get out of that storm? *(Pause for response.)* That's right, you can crawl under the rock. Suddenly, there's a flood from all the rain. What do you do? *(Pause for response.)* Yes, you crawl up on the rock, away from danger. Now something nasty is after you; what do you do? *(Pause for response.)* Sure, you hide behind the rock. Someone could throw other rocks at you, and you'd be protected.

Nothing is quite as changeless as a rock, and nothing is quite as solid as a rock. That's why the Bible calls God our rock again and again. The Bible says that God is the rock of our salvation.

Does a rock change? *(Pause for response.)* No! God doesn't change either. He said, "I am the Lord, I do not change." He will always be there for you.

Is a big rock good protection? *(Pause for response.)* About the best there is. But God is more solid than a rock and bigger than we can ever imagine. And he has promised to protect *and* care for us. That's much more than a big rock can do.

(Hold up the rock.) But a rock can remind you of God, can't it? This rock won't change by itself as long as we're alive. If it were bigger it would be super protection. This week keep your eyes open for some big rocks. And when you see them, think of God, who will never change, who will always be solid as a rock.

Out of Sight

Scripture: The eyes of the LORD are everywhere, keeping watch on the wicked and the good (Prov. 15:3).

Concept: We are never out of God's sight.

Object: A tiny stick figure, drawn on a piece of paper. The drawing should be too small for the children to see. (*Note:* It would be nice to have one tiny drawing for each child.)

Song: "You Cannot Hide from God."

I brought one little thing with me today. You brought most of what we're going to use! Everybody came with two eyes, right? We're going to exercise our eyes today as we talk about them.

Everybody look at me for a minute. Can you see what I'm doing? *(Wave your arms as you ask the question and pause for response.)* Good! You can all see that I'm waving my arms.

Now try this. Keep looking at me, and try to look at (your minister *or* someone obviously out of their line of vision) at the same time. Don't move your head, just look at us both at the same time. *(Pause while they try.)* Can you do that? *(Shake your head as you ask and pause for response.)* Of course not! No one can see in two directions *(indicate two different directions)* at the same time. No one can look at two people when they're so far apart.

No one? I know one person who can look in all directions at the same time. Do you think God can see here *(indicate a direction)* and here *(indicate another direction)* at the same time? *(Nod your head and pause for response.)* Of course. Only God can look in different directions at the same time.

(Hold up the picture.) Can you see this picture of a person? *(Pause for response.)* No? You can't see this person? What's wrong? Is the picture too small? *(Pause for response.)* I thought it would be too small. I can hardly see it, and I'm holding it. No one can see something this small.

No one? I know one person who can see things this small and much, much smaller. Do you think God can see this picture? *(Pause for response.)* Yes, he can. God can see everything, no matter how small it is.

Now, without getting up, try to see if there's anyone walking around outside of church. Look through the wall over there. *(Point to a wall and pause.)* Can you see through that wall? *(Pause for response.)* Of course not! No one can see through walls.

No one? I know one person who can see through walls. Who is that? *(Pause for response.)* Of course! God can see through walls. God can see through anything.

Now pretend that it's night and there are no lights on in here. Would you be able to see me? *(Pause for response.)* No, not without lights! No one can see in the dark.

No one? Who can see in the dark? *(Pause for response.)* God can! God can see in the dark and in the light. He can see through walls and through anything else. He can see big things and small things. He can even look all over at the same time! He can see everybody in the whole wide world, all at the same time!

And he does! The Bible tells us that the eyes of the Lord are everywhere, keeping watch on everyone. That means that God is watching us right now. When you go back to your seat, he will watch you; and when you go home, he'll watch over you; and when you go to bed tonight, he'll watch over you.

Do you know why he watches—(and watches over)—you? Because he loves you! You are so precious to God that he doesn't want to let you out of his sight. So he doesn't. God can see anywhere, so he always watches you and watches over you.

(Hold up the picture one more time.) Some people think that they look this tiny to God. Now you know that you don't. You look just like *(indicate the group of children)* you! No matter where you go, how many people are around, or how dark it is, God will always be able to see you. He'll always be watching over you in love!

Option

(If you have a picture for each child, add this paragraph.)

Just to remind you of our lesson this week, I have a picture for each of you. Take it home and hang it

Turn On the Light!

Scripture: Your word is a lamp to my feet and a light for my path (Ps. 119:105).

Concept: The Bible tells us how to live.

Objects: A flashlight and a Bible. (*Note:* Even though this lesson is especially effective in the dark, both darkness and daylight versions are given here.)

Song: "Stepping in the Light," "The Light of the World Is Jesus."

Who can tell me what this is? (*Hold up the flashlight. Pause for response.*) Of course, it's a flashlight.

What are some things you use a flashlight for? (*Pause for response.*) Yes, you use it to find your way in the dark. You can use it to look into dark closets or shine it out in your yard at night. The best use is to light your path, to find your way. Sometimes a light like this flashlight is absolutely necessary to find your way.

Option 1

(*If it is dark, say,*) Let me show you what I mean. We're going to turn off all the lights for a minute.

You stay right here; I'll be right here with you. Everybody will stay in his or her place, but it's going to be quite dark. Are you ready? OK. Will someone please turn off all the lights?

There's quite a difference, isn't there? It's almost impossible to see in the dark.

Now pretend, just pretend, that I told you to go back to your seats in the dark. You wouldn't be able to find your way, would you? You'd probably stumble and fall over things. You'd never find your seat. You can't find your way in the dark.

(Turn on the flashlight.) That helps, doesn't it? At least there's a little bit of light. Maybe if I gave each of you a flashlight you'd be able to find your way. Each of you would need your own light to make sure you wouldn't bump into anything and to find your seat. A flashlight is absolutely necessary to find your way in the dark. *(Turn the flashlight off.)*

Let's turn the lights back on now, please.

Option 2

(If it is daylight, say,) Pretend for a minute that it's night time. We have no lights; it's as dark as it can be in here. There's no way to turn on the lights, and yet I tell you to go back to your seats.

Would you be able to find your way in the dark? *(Pause for response.)* No! You'd probably stumble and fall over things. You'd never find your seat. You just can't find your way in the dark.

But if I gave you each a flashlight, and you turned it on like this *(turn on the flashlight)*, would you be able to find your way? *(Pause for response.)* Probably.

You could shine the flashlight ahead of you *(demonstrate)* to find your seat. And you could shine the light down at your feet *(demonstrate)* so you wouldn't stumble. A flashlight would be absolutely necessary for you to find your way. *(Turn the flashlight off.)*

Continue Lesson

The Bible *(hold up the Bible)* is just like this flashlight. The Bible is absolutely necessary for you to find your way.

The Bible says that it, God's Word, is a lamp for our feet and a light for our path. Of course, God's Word doesn't show us the way back to our seats. A flashlight keeps us from stumbling over things and helps us find our seats. God's Word, the Bible, keeps us from making mistakes in our lives and shows us the way to live.

In the Bible God tells us a lot about the way to live. Does God say that we should obey our parents? *(Pause for response.)* Yes! That's like a light on your path. You may think, "Should I obey Mom and Dad?" The Bible says *(flash the flashlight once)*, "Children, obey your parents" (Eph. 6:1).

Should we love God? *(Pause for response.)* Yes! The Bible says *(flash the flashlight)*, "Love the Lord your God with all your heart and with all your soul and with all your mind" (Matt. 22:37).

Should we love one another? *(Pause for response.)* Yes! The Bible says *(flash the flashlight)*, "Love your neighbor as yourself" (Luke 10:27).

149

Should we believe in Jesus? *(Pause for response.)* Yes! The Bible says *(flash the flashlight)*, "Believe in the Lord Jesus, and you will be saved" (Acts 16:31).

How should we treat each other? *(Pause for response.)* The Bible says *(flash the flashlight)*, "Do to others as you would have them do to you" (Luke 6:31).

That's what the Bible means when it says God's Word is a light for your path. God's Word shows you the way to go in life just like this flashlight shows you the way to go in the dark.

I'd like you to try a little experiment tonight. Before you go to bed, find a flashlight. Go into your bedroom, pull the shades, close the door, and turn off the light. Then use the flashlight to find your way to bed. When you get there, you can think about how the Bible is like that flashlight, only much better. The flashlight helped you find your way to bed. The Bible helps you find your way through life!

Clouds and Cares

Scripture: God has said, "Never will I leave you, never will I forsake you." So we say with confidence, "The Lord is my helper; I will not be afraid. What can man do to me?" (Heb. 13:5–6). And we know that in all things God works for the good of those who love him (Rom. 8:28).

Concept: God will always be near to help with problems and turn circumstances to our good.

Object: A picture of clouds, or a cloudy day (if the children can see the clouds). If the children cannot see real clouds, use option 1.

Song: "No, Never Alone."

Option 1

I sketched a little picture of what we see in the sky quite often. *(Hold up the cloud picture.)* Can anyone tell me what it is? *(Pause for response.)* Yes, it's a picture of clouds. Let's pretend for a minute that it's a cloudy day today.

Option 2

(If the children can see real clouds, say,) It's a cloudy day today, isn't it? *(Point towards the window.)* It's so cloudy that we won't see much sun.

Continue Lesson

We can't see the sun today, can we? The clouds are in the way. Is the sun really gone? Has it dropped out of the sky? *(Shake your head as you ask and pause for response.)* No! It hasn't disappeared forever. It's still up in the sky. We just can't see it because the clouds are in the way.

If we could fly right through the clouds, would we see the sun? *(Pause for response.)* Of course we would. The sun is shining right above the clouds. The clouds are in our way, so it's just down here that we can't see the sun shining. The sun is up in the sky every day. Once in a while the clouds get in our way so that we can't see it.

But clouds aren't all bad, are they? What do some clouds bring us? *(Pause for response or prompt them with questions.)* How about dark rain clouds? What do they bring? Of course, clouds bring us rain. The whole world needs rain. Plants couldn't live without water, could they? When it's too dry we pray for rain. So those dark clouds sometimes bring us good things, even if we don't like them very much.

Sometimes it's hard to see the whole picture when we're sitting below the clouds. *(Point toward the window or hold up the picture.)* We just have to remember two things. First, is the sun still up there? *(Pause for response.)* Of course it is; the clouds are in the way, that's all. And second, do these clouds bring good things sometimes? *(Pause for response.)* They do! We may not like the rain, but in the end it's good for us.

Our problems or worries are just like little clouds. Let me explain that. Sometimes our problems or worries can make us forget about God. Or we're so worried that we think maybe God forgot about us. But God has promised never to leave us. He will never, ever disappear. He will always be near us. He will never forget us. So, even if we worry that God forgot us, or even if we forget about God, is he still near to us? *(Nod and pause for response.)* Yes, that's what he promised.

Just as the clouds sometimes cover the sun *(hold up the picture or point to the window)* from our view, so our problems sometimes cover up God from our view. But just as the sun is always there, so God is always there. He promised never to leave us.

And just as the clouds bring us good things sometimes, so do our problems. God has also promised that. God said that he would take our problems and somehow turn them to our good. That's hard to understand.

It's like when it's raining and really icky weather, we don't like it at all, but we know the rain is good for the earth. If we have problems and worries, we can't see how they're good for us at all, but God promised to make them good for us. So we trust God.

God loves us and doesn't want us sad. God wants to shine love on us all the time. That's why he promised never to leave us and to work all our problems to our good in the end. Sometimes those problems and worries get between us and God, just as

Whiter than Snow

Scripture: Wash me, and I will be whiter than snow (Ps. 51:7).

Concept: Jesus takes away our sins.

Object: A "snowflake" cut from white paper. (*Note:* If you live in a warm climate you may want to have a copy of the flake, uncut, for each child. Trace your original flake on white paper, or use a copy machine.)

Song: "Whiter than Snow."

Does this look like a snowflake to you? *(Hold up the snowflake. Pause for response.)* I hope so. I tried to make a snowflake for us to look at so that we could talk about snow. *(If there's snow on the ground add,)* We see plenty of snow outside this time of the year.

I love snow, don't you? When it first falls, it's so soft and fluffy and white. (*Or* I think I'd really like snow, don't you? In pictures it always looks so soft and fluffy and white.) I know that it gets dirty after a few days, but new snow is (*or* seems to be) so clean and white.

(Hold up the snowflake.) This is white, but I think that snow is even whiter. Can you think of anything

that's whiter than snow? Is milk whiter than snow? *(Pause for response.)* Is this paper whiter than snow? *(Pause for response.)* Is a little white sheep whiter than snow? *(Pause for response.)* Can you think of anything that's whiter than snow? *(Pause for response. Repeat any individual responses.)*

There is one thing whiter than snow. The Bible says that God makes us whiter than snow! It says, "Wash me, and I will be whiter than snow." Does that mean that our skin is whiter than this? *(Hold up the snowflake.)* Or whiter than real snow? *(Shake your head and pause for response.)* No! The Bible is using picture language.

Whiter than snow means that there are no spots or stains. "Spots" and "stains" are picture language for sins and bad things. If we have no spots or stains, we have no sins or bad things. When God makes us whiter than snow, he takes away all the sins and bad things we do. He looks at us, and in picture language, we are "whiter than snow."

Who makes us whiter than snow? Who died on the cross to take away our sins? *(Pause for response.)* Yes, Jesus! If we love Jesus, he takes away our sins.

In picture language you say that Jesus "washes away all our spots and stains." He makes us "clean" inside, "whiter than snow."

(Hold up the snowflake.) This is picture language too, isn't it? It isn't really a snowflake, but it can make you think of snow.

Option 1

(If you have no snowflakes for the children and there is no snow, say,) You may want to try what I did this

week and make yourself a snowflake. It's fun to do. As you make the flake, you can remember God's picture language: God will wash you whiter than snow. That means that Jesus takes away your sins.

Option 2

(If you have no snowflakes for the children and there is snow, say,) You don't really need a picture language snowflake, do you? There's plenty of snow outside right now. When you look at it this week, it can remind you of God's picture language: God will wash you whiter than snow. That means that Jesus takes away your sins.

Option 3

(If you have snowflakes for the children, say,) I have a snowflake for each of you today. I haven't cut them out; you must do that. When you do, you can think of how that flake is picture language for snow. That will remind you of God's picture language: God will wash you whiter than snow. That means that Jesus takes away your sins.

46

Labeled with Love

Scripture: And live a life of love, just as Christ loved us (Eph. 5:2).

Concept: Christians should be known by their love.

Objects: A few articles of clothing with manufacturers' labels still in or on them. (*Note:* This works best with well-known labels such as Nike and Reebok. This example is done with a shoe and a T-shirt.)

Song: "They Will Know We Are Christians by Our Love."

Some of you may recognize this brand of shoe right away. *(Hold up the shoe.)* Maybe some of you know the label or recognize what it looks like. Can anyone tell me what brand of shoe this is? *(Pause for response.)* That's right, it's a Reebok. (*Or* A teenager probably could tell you right away that it's a Reebok.)

I don't know much about athletic shoes, but I knew right away that this was a Reebok. How did I know that? *(Pause for response.)* That's right, it's written right on the shoe. *(Point to the word.)* Right here it says "Reebok."

I don't know a Reebok from a Nike, but I bought these shoes because I figured they were pretty good. Reebok is a famous brand; people tell me it's a good shoe.

In fact, some people will buy only Reeboks. They look for the Reebok label and get those shoes.

(Hold up the T-shirt.) Here's another well-known label. It advertises itself right on the shirt. What does this say? *(Point to the name of the shirt.)* Can anyone tell me what kind of T-shirt this is? *(Pause for response.)* That's right, it's a (kind of shirt). (*Or* A teenager probably could tell you right away that it's a _____.)

I don't know much about T-shirts, but I knew right away that this is a _____. How did I know that? *(Pause for response.)* That's right, it's written right on the shirt. *(Point to the word.)* Right here it says, "_____."

I don't know a _____ from a (name of another T-shirt), but I got this T-shirt because I figured it was pretty good. _____ is a famous brand; people tell me it's a good T-shirt.

In fact, some people will buy only _____ T-shirts. They look for the _____ label and get that kind of T-shirt.

Labels often tell us exactly what kind of clothes we're buying. You look at the label and know if you have something really good or not. In fact, labels are so important to some people that they wear those labels where everyone can see them. They're proud that their shoes carry the Reebok, or their T-shirt carries the _____, label.

I think labels in clothes can help us sometimes, but they don't really make a big difference to me.

There is one label that does make a big difference to me, and it should make a big difference to you, too. We all wear that label every day. This label's not on our clothes, it's on us. Can anyone tell me what label we all wear? *(Pause for response. You may have to prompt them with a few questions.)* If you are a follower of Jesus Christ, you are called what? We are all called Christians, aren't we? That's because we believe in Jesus Christ.

We all wear the C-H-R-I-S-T-I-A-N *(pretend you're writing it across your chest or on your shoes, depending on what clothing articles you've used)* label. That spells "Christian." Everybody knows that we are Christians. We are labeled with Jesus Christ's name. That's the best label in the world. We can carry the Christian label proudly.

There's one thing that the whole world looks for when they see the Christian label, and that's love. Does Jesus love us? *(Nod and pause for response.)* Do we love Jesus? *(Pause for response.)* Should we love each other? *(Pause for response.)* Yes, love is the most important thing in a Christian's life. The Bible tells us that we should live a life of love, because Christ loved us.

Do you remember what Jesus said about love? Who should we love with all our hearts? *(Point upward and pause for response.)* Yes, we should love the Lord our God with all our hearts. Who should we love as ourselves? *(Point to the children and pause for response.)* We should love our neighbors as ourselves.

If we are Christians, we should be very loving people. Christians are known for their love. That's part of the Christian label.

I'd like you to try something tonight when you get ready for bed. Maybe Mom or Dad or an adult in your house can remind you of this. *(Hold up the clothes.)* Look for the labels in your clothes. Someone can read them to you. Are any of them famous labels? See if any of the labels in your clothes mean anything to you. Then, when you say your nightly prayers, ask God to help you wear the label "Christian" proudly with love.

Your Ticket to Heaven

Scripture: Believe in the Lord Jesus, and you will be saved (Acts 16:31).

Concept: Only belief in Jesus will admit us to heaven.

Objects: A ticket or tickets; imitation tickets with "JESUS" written on each, one for each child.

Song: "'Tis So Sweet to Trust in Jesus."

I have a few really precious pieces of paper here; can you see them? *(Show them the real tickets.)* Can anyone tell me what they are? *(Pause for response.)* Yes, they're tickets.

These are tickets to (<u>the event</u>). I really wanted to go to (<u>the event</u>), so I went out and bought these tickets. The tickets were almost gone when I bought these. I guess that a lot of people want to go to (<u>the event</u>).

If I didn't have these tickets, would I be able to get into (<u>the event</u>)? *(Shake your head and pause for response.)* No! You absolutely need a ticket to get in. Without a ticket, I couldn't get in.

That's because there are just so many seats at (<u>the site of the event</u>). So there are just that many tickets. When the tickets are sold out, no one else can get in. If you don't have a ticket, you don't have a seat; so you can't even get in.

There are many places where you need a ticket to get in. If you go to (<u>name of a local sporting event</u>) you must show a ticket to get in. If you go to (<u>name of a local concert</u>) you need a ticket. You need a ticket to get into (<u>an amusement park</u>) or into (<u>a museum</u>). Can you think of any other places that you need a ticket to get into? *(Pause for response. If no responses are forthcoming, list a few more—a current fair, a show, some event, or some building.)*

You need a ticket to each one of these places, don't you? There are just so many seats or so much space, and if you don't have a ticket you don't get in.

There's one place we haven't mentioned yet where you need a ticket to get in. Can you think of what it is? Let me give you some hints *(pause after each hint)*: It's someplace we all want to go to live forever and ever. . . . When a Christian dies, we often say he or she went to where? . . . Often we say that's where God lives. . . . Jesus came down from where to earth? . . . That's right, heaven!

Did you know that you need a ticket to get into heaven? Every person (<u>or name of a recently deceased person</u>) that we said "went to heaven" had a ticket. Nobody gets into heaven without a ticket. I'll need a ticket to get into heaven. You'll need a ticket to get into heaven.

But you don't have to worry. I have your tickets right here. *(Show them the imitation tickets and pass them out. Continue to speak as you distribute them.)* Here's one ticket for each of you. Everybody needs one, but one is enough. Your ticket is free; you don't have to pay for it. The price has been paid already. There's just one thing that you must do to make your ticket good.

Look at your ticket; there's one word printed on it. Can anyone tell me what that one word says? *(Pause for response.)* That's right, it says "JESUS" in big letters.

The one thing you must do to get into heaven is believe in Jesus. God says in the Bible that if you believe in Jesus, if you love Jesus, you will be saved. When you die you will go to heaven to live with him. Jesus is your ticket into heaven.

God also says in the Bible that Jesus is the *only* way into heaven. If you don't believe in Jesus, if you don't love him, you won't go to heaven. Jesus is your *only* ticket into heaven.

The nice thing about these tickets into heaven is that there are plenty of them. God never runs out of tickets. There's room in heaven for everybody. Everyone who believes in Jesus, everyone who loves Jesus, will go to heaven.

Do you love Jesus? *(Pause and nod your head.)* Then you will go to heaven. You have your ticket.

You don't really need those little pieces of paper I gave you. I just used them as a reminder to believe in Jesus and love him. You may take your paper ticket home with you. Use it this week to remind you about Jesus, your real ticket into heaven.

If you lose this paper ticket, don't worry. Jesus is your real "ticket." You won't lose him, and he won't lose you, as long as you believe in and love him.

Pine Cone People

Scripture: Be careful not to do your "acts of righteousness" before men, to be seen by them (Matt. 6:1).

Concept: Do kind acts quietly, to please God.

Object: A pine cone.

Who can tell me what this is? *(Hold up the pine cone so all can see it. Pause for response.)* Of course, it's a pine cone. Everyone knows a pine cone when they see one.

Can anyone see something special about this pine cone? *(Turn the cone around slowly so they can see all sides. Shake your head as you ask the question to elicit the right response.)* It looks like any other pine cone, doesn't it? This is just an ordinary, brown cone. I can't see anything special about it.

But there is something special about this pine cone. In fact, there's something special about all pine cones. Not many people know this secret of the pine cones that I'm going to tell you. Most people think this is just a brown pine cone.

(Talk very slowly, as if you're telling them a great secret:) Inside this cone, under these scales that are still shut tightly, *(point to some of the brown scales that*

are still closed, folded down near the cone), there are seeds for whole new pine trees. When the scales open *(point to an open scale)*, the seeds beneath them drop to the ground and can sprout into new trees. Pine cones are very good and very important in a forest, because they hold the seeds for new pine trees.

Not many people know that a pine cone holds all those seeds, because the seeds are hidden. They don't know that a pine cone drops pine seeds, because the seeds drop secretly. They think a cone is just a brown cone; they don't know how good and important a pine cone is.

Jesus wants us to act like pine cones. That sounds funny, doesn't it? Let me explain.

Jesus said that we should do kind acts quietly. He said to be careful that we don't do them just so that other people will see them. He said to do them in secret. Jesus even said, "Do not announce it with trumpets." He wants us to be quietly kind to please him.

In other words, don't do this: *(Stand up tall, spread out your arms, throw your head back and say loudly,)* "Ta Da! Look everybody, I'm doing something kind!" Rather, he wants us to act quietly.

Who can tell me a kind act you can do quietly? *(Pause for response. Repeat all responses and elaborate on them somewhat.)* How about sharing your toys with a friend? You don't have to tell everyone, "Hey, I shared my toys with Jimmy." Just do it quietly. How about being kind to someone who has no friends? Do you have to make a big deal of it? Of course not. If you help a friend do a chore, you don't have to tell anyone about it. Just do it quietly.

The idea is to do a kind act, not to have everyone praise you. God wants us to be kind, and Jesus tells us to do it quietly. If you do that, you're a pine cone person. *(Hold up the pine cone again.)* You may not look like anything special. But in secret, you're dropping seeds of kindness. *(Point to an open scale.)* You're quiet about it to please God, not people.

Next time you see a pine cone, you can remember that God wants you to be a pine cone person. He wants you to do your kind acts quietly to please him.

49

What Do You Say?

Scripture: Sing and make music in your heart to the Lord, always giving thanks to God the Father for everything, in the name of our Lord Jesus Christ (Eph. 5:19–20).

Concept: We should joyfully thank God for everything.

Object: A thank-you card. (*Note:* Use the option if giving this lesson on Thanksgiving Day.)

Song: "Thank You, Lord, for Saving My Soul."

Can you all see this card? (*Hold up the card.*) Can anyone tell me what kind of card this is? Is it a birthday card? A Christmas card? Can you read what it says? (*Pause for response.*) This is a thank-you card. It says, (*read the card*).

Sometimes we send formal thank-you cards like this. If a person gives me a present or does something really nice for me, I may send them a thank-you card like this. Especially if I don't see that person very often, I want to make sure they know I appreciate the gift, so I'll send a thank-you card. Sometimes people send cards like this, but not very often.

We always say thank you for things, though, don't we? When someone gives you a gift, what do you say? *(Pause for response.)* Of course, you say, "Thank you." When someone does something especially nice for you, what do you say? *(Pause for response.)* Yes, you say, "Thank you." When your parents do something special for you, what do you say? *(Pause for response.)* You say, "Thank you." When anyone gives you something or does something special for you, what do you say? *(Pause for response.)* You always say, "Thank you."

There is someone who is always giving you gifts and always doing good things for you, someone besides your parents. Do you know who I'm talking about? *(Pause for response. You may have to lead them with a few questions.)* Who makes sure that enough food grows? Who put the sun to shine in the sky? Who gave us flowers to enjoy? Who gave us wonderful bodies? Yes, God!

God gives us everything that we need. God says that he loves us. God sent Jesus to save us. God gave us our bodies to work just right for us. God gives us every new day.

Do you remember to say thank you to God? Sometimes we need little reminders, don't we? That's why I'm reminding you today. We should always say thank you to God for everything that he gives us.

The Bible gives us a little reminder, too. The Bible tells us to give thanks to God the Father for everything.

How can we give our thanks to God? *(Pause for response.)* Can we sing our thanks? Singing is a really joyful way to say thanks to God. Can we just say, "Thank you, God"? Of course! A quick "Thank you" once in a while is good. Can we remember to say thanks when we pray? It's really important to say thanks when we pray. We can do all of those things. The important thing is to remember to always say thanks to God.

Option

That's part of the reason it's Thanksgiving Day today. Today reminds us to say thanks to God for everything that he gives us. Today is a formal thank-you day *(hold up the card)*, sort of like this formal thank-you card. But it reminds us to say thank you to God every day.

Continue Lesson

To help you remember to say thank you, I'd like you to do something special today. Listen to the songs we sing in church. Listen especially for some "Thank you's." Then, listen very closely to the prayers we pray. Listen for those "Thank you's." Then, listen very closely to the prayers your parents say at home. If you pray aloud before a meal, listen very closely to what you are saying. Listen for the "Thank you's."

After all that listening *(hold up the card)*, you won't need a formal card to remind you to say thank you to God. You'll hear those "Thank you's." And they can remind you that in your own prayers and songs, you should say what? *(Pause for response.)* Yes, you should say, "Thank you, God" for everything that he gives you.

50

The Best Gift of All

Scripture: Thanks be to God for his indescribable gift! (2 Cor. 9:15).

Concept: Jesus is God's gift to us.

Objects: A few gift-wrapped objects; a picture of Jesus or a Jesus from a nativity set, in a gift-wrapped box. (*Note:* Put the gifts in a noticeable place before the service.)

Song: "Thank You, Lord, for Saving My Soul."

You probably all saw these gifts when you came into church this morning. This time of the year we see lots of wrapped gifts. How many of you have some gifts like this at home? *(Pause for response.)* If there aren't any now, there probably will be some soon. It's a season to give gifts.

That's why I brought these along; this is a good time to talk about gifts. Most of these are pretend gifts, just to help us think about gifts. So let's unwrap them and see what we have.

(Hold up a gift.) This is to me from _____. *(Unwrap it and show the children.)* Look, a _____. How nice! I can really use this. At least right now I can. It will probably (break, wear out, go bad, shrink) someday.

This gift doesn't last forever, but it surely is nice right now. Thank you, _____.

(Continue in this manner with all the gifts except the picture of Jesus. Comment on how nice they are, but that they'll someday wear out. You may even want to add one gift that you can't use but can exchange. Always mention thanking someone for the gift.)

Gifts are very nice to receive. They may wear out someday, or you may not really like one too much. But when someone gives you a gift it shows that they were thinking of you. We always say thank you for our gifts.

(Hold up the last box.) We've got one gift left. This is the best gift of all. And, do you know what? It's to all of us, and it's from God. What do you think is in here? *(Pause for response. Repeat their responses.)*

Let's unwrap it and find out. *(Unwrap the gift.)* You were right *(if a child has guessed it was Jesus)*! It's Jesus! Of course it's Jesus.

(Hold up the picture or figure.) This is absolutely the best gift of all time! God gave us Jesus to save us from our sins. We can do without these other gifts, but without Jesus we're lost. These other gifts will wear out, but Jesus will be our savior forever. Jesus is the perfect gift, God's gift to us.

What do we say when we get a gift? *(Pause for response.)* Yes, we say, "Thank you." Maybe we should say thank you to God right now.

Thank you, God, for giving us Jesus to save us from our sins. Jesus is the best gift of all, from you to us. Amen.

How many of you think that you'll receive some gifts at Christmas this year? *(Pause for response.)* We'll probably all get a gift or two. But we know that we already have the best gift of all, don't we? We have Jesus.

In fact, all these other gifts at Christmas are really here to remind us of Jesus. God gave us a wonderful gift; Jesus was born on the first Christmas. We celebrate God's gift by giving each other gifts.

So this year your gifts can remind you of the best gift of all *(hold up the picture or figure of Jesus)*: Jesus! And, when you say thank you for a gift *(indicate the other gifts)*, add another thank you. Say thank you to God for sending Jesus, the best gift of all.